Sailing Above Lobsters

A Summer's Cruise in Maine

by

Clifford McKay

North
Country
Press

Sailing Above Lobsters

Copyright © 2014 by Clifford McKay

ISBN 978-0-945980-85-8

Library of Congress Control Number: 2014955450

Cover photo and design by Erin Weiffenbach

North Country Press
Unity, Maine

"*Any avid sailor to Maine can tell why the coast is so attractive to cruisers. The challenge of the weather and the rocky shores, the variety provided by the ebb and flow of the tides, the beauty of the unspoiled islands, the sense of timelessness, the independence and self-reliance of the Maine people, their wit and good humor and peculiar idiom and accent....all these help, of course, but foremost is the evidence of hardships conquered and dangers averted, evidence of a people's heroism. That's what the Maine coast is all about.*"

"*Avelinda*" by Thomas Cabot, p. 152

Introduction

The chill wind seeped through all our layers. We wore high-tech underwear, shirt and pants, fleece, and foul weather gear, but that was barely enough to keep us warm. Bezy, my wife and shipmate, brought up the throw rugs from below to help insulate us from the cold, wet cockpit cushions. We warmed ourselves with hot chocolate and peanut butter crackers as the Isles of Shoals disappeared over the horizon astern.

In spite of the cold, we were excited to finally draw abeam of Cape Porpoise as we sailed parallel to the coast, about three miles off. At last, Cape Elizabeth emerged through the haze. We entered the location for each of the three green cans that mark the ledges of the Cape in our Global Positioning System and rounded each in turn. As we bore off to the northwest, into the ship channel that goes up towards Portland, the wind gusted to twenty-five knots. No matter, we would soon be in the protection of the headland, sheltered from both the wind and the sea. Our decision to go, despite the threatening weather, turned out to be a good one.

The clouds grew darker as we entered Portland harbor. If the rain could hold off just a bit longer... We hailed the Centerboard Yacht Club, across the harbor from downtown Portland, picked up a mooring, and ducked below just as the rain blew in from the west in wind driven sheets. We crashed for five hours of sound sleep, our bodies reacting as if we'd been underway all night on the ocean. But at last, we're here! We've made it to Maine! The Isles of Shoals are really Maine, but here in Portland, on the edge of Casco Bay it feels more like we've arrived. It's been a passage of fits and starts in unusual weather from our home base in St Petersburg, Florida, but our thirty-two-foot sloop *Ceilidh* has brought us safely back...back to Maine.

When the Isles of Shoals disappeared below the horizon four years ago, we promised ourselves we would return. The scent of the spruce, balsam, and pine, the rugged beauty of the rock-lined coast with the waves crashing against the rocks, the ebb and flow of the tides, the unspoiled islands, the deep clear water, and the independence and self-reliance of its people, all drew us back with a siren's call. But to sail here requires tenacity and a firm control of your vessel, not to mention the challenge of the weather's incessant unpredictability. If you look away, or let up, you can be in trouble in an instant. The currents, the rock ledges, the wind shifts, and the ever-present fog require you to keep your wits about you and maintain great patience and determination to get where you're going. No other form of travel, and no other approach to this fascinating state is quite the same. Only viewed from the water does Maine come alive in all of its maritime splendor. Despite the challenges and difficulties, it's exhilarating to cruise here in the rugged beauty of this area, attempting to understand its bewitching charm and why its challenges seem more enticing than threatening.

Chapter 1

Welcome to Maine…and to Fog

The next morning as we looked out the ports, our whole world had shrunk. Portland had disappeared and the nearby yacht club as well. All we saw were the shadowy outlines of the seven boats moored close around us, masked with a gray shroud. The fog curtained off everything else and encapsulated us in a cocoon of silence. I never saw the "little cat feet" on which the fog crept in, but there must have been a bunch of them. It was time for a leisurely cup of coffee and to wait. On a boat, wind, tide, and fog set the schedule. One must push back the hurry-hurry of the 21st century and enjoy the moment. Sailing is a kickback, take it easy and relax sport. As I sipped my coffee and dozed, I heard, or at least I thought I heard a lobster whisper laconically, "Welcome to Maine."

When the fog lifted about 11o'clock, as it usually does when the morning sun burns it off, the yacht club launch took us across the harbor to explore Portland on a trolley tour, an excellent way we've found to get an overview of a city and to identify places of special interest to visit later. A well informed local high school teacher was the driver. He was proud of his city and happy to show it off.

"Portland is the closest ice-free port to Europe," he noted. "Oil destined for Canada arrives here, and is then sent by pipeline to Montreal. The oil rig they're building over there, will be towed around the tip of Florida and placed in the Gulf of Mexico when it is finished."

He pointed out the L.L.Bean factory outlet a couple of blocks from the town center and the new Public Market that sells a wide range of Maine edibles. After the tour, we located Hamilton Marine and picked up several parts we'd been searching for. We stumbled upon an old line chandlery, Chase Leavitt & Co, and it was having a sale. Such classic marine stores are always interesting and hard to find. We saw a bronze lead line, jib sheet blocks made of wood with metal straps and oil burning running lights, all reminding us of the long rich heritage of the sea.

I spotted an ice cream place where I could indulge my long-time habit, and we passed the Museum of Fine Arts that brings special exhibits of noted artists like Robert Indiana, Picasso, and John Singer Sargent to Portland. We checked out how to get to the airport and had lunch at Gritty's, washed down with some of their microbrewery beer before returning to the boat. We learned a lot about Portland and identified several places we wanted to visit again. That night, a rock band concert blasted us out of the cabin at a distance of more than half a mile. It lasted until 2 o'clock in the morning.

Next morning we dropped our mooring and headed to Peaks Island on the southeast corner of the harbor. We cruised slowly through the anchorage, found a spot, dropped the hook and went ashore. Peaks Island's high bluffs overlook the Portland harbor. The mix of year-round residents and summer tourists have only a short ferry ride from Portland. The anchorage's only limitation is that it lies alongside a major thoroughfare used by all the pleasure and commercial boats from Portland heading out into Casco Bay. The wakes they caused were constant and sometimes large enough to be exciting. Throughout the day we maintained a "secure for sea" mode with everything battened down until the last boats went home at dark.

Ashore, we found the Peaks Island Fest in full swing. The festival managed to take over much of the small island from the ferry dock, past all the shops all the way up to the Fire Station and the Church. It's for locals to celebrate together before the tourist hoards descend for the summer. A parade passed by, including most of the island children on their bikes, trikes, and American Flyer wagons. The fest's king and queen were dressed in street clothes and lobster fishing gear. Their royal carriage was the back of a pickup truck. No need to get too fancy. A golf cart decorated with fish, shells and netting carried a rather elderly looking gray haired mermaid, her tail draped casually off the back. (Later, at the church pie-eating contest, we discovered that the mermaid sans wig was actually a redheaded young man.) The parade wound back and forth, passing us at least four times. The island is small, and they didn't have a lot of space to work with so they circled. The tykes on tricycles were tiring. A few dropped out each lap, most of them as they passed the ice cream parlor. A treat quickly revived them. The fire department had open house, providing calendars and gold stick-on fireman's badges for the children. We were disappointed that we arrived too late for the Garage Sale, the hamburgers on the grill, and the T-shirt stamping. It was small town America at its best, showing off and having fun.

A local man told us with a great deal of pride about his role in the Fest. "I arranged for all the dignitaries, raised $2000 and organized everything. My wife and I provided the hot dogs, potato salad, baked beans and drinks, free of charge. It's important to all of us to have this time together. We're so glad you came to join us." He was proud of his community and happy to share it.

"Oh, and be sure to come back tomorrow morning for the Lion's Club pancake breakfast," he said. "Everyone will be there, and you can meet lots of people."

"We'll do just that," we responded.

We dinghied ashore the next morning for pancakes. The whole island was there. The excuse was to eat pancakes but the real reason they came was to visit and chat. A number of people introduced themselves and asked where we were from. They were surprised when we pointed to *Ceilidh* riding gently at anchor in the harbor. Two ladies sat beside us and told us all about the history and the great qualities of their island. The population more than doubles during July and August when the tourists arrive. They love Peaks Island and are very proud of it. We found this same friendliness and unabashed pride everywhere we went.

After eating our fill of fluffy blueberry pancakes, we returned to *Ceilidh*, pulled the anchor, and journeyed the 12 miles to South Freeport, wending our way through the islands of Casco Bay. The sun came out with low lying cumulous clouds and winds were moderate as we sailed between two rows of islands, the typical

Maine layout, where the bays follow the valleys carved by the glaciers. It was picture post card Maine at its best.

Ceilidh at sunset off Peak's Island

Chapter 2

South Freeport and Freeport

Brewer's South Freeport Marina had a mooring available out at the entrance of the river just across from Pound of Tea Island. These are new moorings, added to an already crowded mooring field. Pound of Tea is a very small island right at the entrance to the Harraseeket River with an equally small house perched on a rock squeezed in tight between the island's three trees. Nowadays, moorings abound in the river making navigation upstream to Freeport a serpentine path at best. It's a challenge to find the channel as it winds its way through all the mooring balls and boats at the river entrance. The channel marks are often hidden behind the moored boats until after you've passed them.

We took the launch ashore and got a cab to L.L.Bean's in Freeport. For Bezy, this is like a pilgrimage to the shrine of shopping. She turned to catalogue shopping early on and was drawn quickly to L.L.Bean's distinctive, practical, quality clothes and gear. Not only do we buy most of our clothes from L.L.Bean but it's also a favorite for our Christmas shopping, fleece for those in the north, wreaths and polo's for those in the south. Bezy's excitement was palpable as she hurried inside to touch and feel, to look and learn about the new fabrics and new colors, and to actually be present at the "home of it all." We've shopped with them so much, I expected "L.L." himself to come out with a personal welcome. As for me, I admired the varnished Old Town canoes and kayaks, the Adirondack chairs, and the array of pocket knives before taking a seat on the bench at the front door where husbands sit and wait for their wives. Bezy came away with very modest purchases. She was satisfied "just to be here," to see the counters and racks of the clothes she loved best and to see the full palette of colors and to connect each to its name, gray heather, beeswax, lapis quartz and bering blue, and to tuck it all away in her memory. It was like a visit to...to...to a shrine.

Along with the original world-renowned outdoor outfitter L.L. Bean, Freeport is home to 150 outlet stores. It has become a shopping haven, designed for "professional shoppers." But it's the L.L.Bean store that captured our interest. It is amazing in both its size and breadth. Their bicycle shop is a whole floor, with tent and camping equipment underneath, not to mention the fly fishing store, or the hunting and gun shop, or the household section, and of course there's shoes, men's and women's clothing, and luggage. This complete offering of outdoor equipment has no locks on the doors. It doesn't need them since it never closes...never, not even Christmas Day or New Year's. Mr. Bean was committed to supplying the hunters and fishermen who needed gear for their early morning starts. He got up at any hour of the night to serve them. As business grew and he was getting up time and again through the night, he decided it wasn't worth returning to bed so he just stayed open all night. Finally, since he was open all the time, he removed the locks and threw away the keys.

There are limits on what we can buy. Our boat is small, and we're out of space for any more stuff. These days, it must either be edible or a boat part to be allowed on aboard.

By the time we'd finished touring L.L.Bean's, we were hungry, so we lunched at Jameson Tavern. In addition to being a quality modern restaurant, it is also a 17th century historical site where the documents of Maine Statehood were signed. As I was eating, I closed my eyes and imagined the restaurant morphed into a dark crowded room filled with smoke and smells from the food cooking in the open fireplace. The air was charged with the tension and excitement of the historic moment. Near the fire, chairs were pulled up to the table where the official documents were laid out, along with the pens for the signers. A few men were standing in the back, over by the bar, still grumbling. For Mainers it had been too long in coming and with too much conflict and turmoil. Maine had been part of Massachusetts and finally, at last, it was to be a state on its own. But statehood had been granted primarily because the country needed a free state to balance Missouri as a slave state. Independent Mainers like things done on their own terms; they don't like to be used to settle someone else's concerns. I opened my eyes, returned to reality, and finished the last of my mussels steamed in wine sauce.

Freeport was vital to England in Colonial times. Trees were shipped from the Maine forests for masts for the Royal Navy. Freeport's streets were laid out so the long tree trunks could make the turn on their way to the harbor. Main Street still has a long sweeping bend in it, a bend designed a long time ago so the masts wouldn't hit the buildings as they turned the corner on the horse-drawn drays. The Harraseeket River was navigable all the way up river so the English ships could load their ungainly cargo at the town wharf.

Returning to the marina in Southport, we discovered the small cafe on the nearby town dock. It draws a big clientele because of its excellent seafood. Our boiled lobster was the best I've ever eaten, the tender, succulent kind that melt in your mouth, accompanied by corn on the cob and slaw. Lobster is certainly one of Maine's enticing contributions. The large picnic tables overlooking the river seat ten or twelve so you get to make new friends as you eat. We met three ladies who had previously lived in Florida. They returned to Maine when their husbands died because they preferred the quality of life here and weren't really troubled by the cold. "The harsh winters don't bother us. They're only an inconvenience," one of them said, "and we know to be careful of our footing on the snow and ice."

We remained on the mooring the next day in order to wash clothes. Our extensive collection of dirty laundry provided a full day's work for the single washer available. So, while the washer was washing and the dryer drying, we found an empty bench and cut each other's hair. We've been doing this for years. It always draws interesting comments from onlookers... "Can I be next?" "Do you really trust him to cut your hair?" "You missed a spot over there!" And, "I can't believe what I'm seeing."

Properly coiffured, we walked around the boatyard to see what we could learn about other boats and what their hulls looked like below the waterline. You don't often get to see the undersides of boats. I dive and clean the bottom of ours, change the sacrificial zincs when needed and watch for when the bottom paint needs another coat. Seeing other hulls gives me perspective on mine.

A rough survey revealed that 70% of local boats, at least those hauled out of the water at Brewer's that day, have line cutters on their propeller shafts to cut the lines of the lobster traps so the lines won't foul the props. I was surprised there were so many using these devices despite the difficulty caused when a propeller or rudder snags a line. If they cut the line, the float drifts away and the trap is lost. The loss of a trap is a significant cost to a lobsterman. It's not always easy to combine the use of the waterways for several purposes like lobster fishing and fast spinning propellers, but it's important for commercial and pleasure boaters to work together.

We chatted with a couple of lobstermen as they worked on their hauled-out boats. One was renewing the extra layer of planking at the side where the traps bang against the hull as they're hauled aboard. He said, "Good white oak works well for this job."

We asked when he would set his traps and what kind of season he was expecting. "The season is looking good. I think you'll have enough lobster to eat," and added, "I hope to start fishing in about a week."

Another lobsterman was finishing the last details prior to a launch later in the day. Both were friendly and genial. They work long and hard, and we appreciate what they bring to the table. Just thinking about lobster made us hungry, so since it was about lunchtime, we had another lobster for lunch at the café.

As we ate, a thick fog rolled in, blanketing the whole harbor. We gasped in surprise. I thought fog was an early morning or late afternoon thing, not for midday. When it lifted about four o'clock, we were surprised again and realized how much we had to learn about fog, one of Maine's most important weather features.

Next day, we arose leisurely, weighed anchor and meandered the fourteen miles back to Portland. It was a six seal day, according to Bezy, when she saw the sixth of these cunning creatures as we wound our way between the islands and lobster pots of Casco Bay. They popped their heads up, looked around, and then dove, rolling up their backs and flipping their tails in the air. They didn't seem disturbed by boats and people. I believe they surfaced more for curiosity, just to check things out. Then, with their curiosity satisfied, they dove again to look for fish.

Chapter 3

A Journey Inland to Fryeburg

From Portland we rented a car and drove inland beside the tree-lined lakes, past the White Mountains, to Fryeburg, Maine, to visit Gina, a daughter of some very good friends. As we passed Sebago Lake State Park, we took time to walk down to the lake and stick our toes in the water. The water was chilly, but it was the first sunny day of summer and everyone was out in force to enjoy it. We understood why they sunbathed and played around the water's edge rather than swam. The water was still very cold.

We took out our lunch and settled down at a picnic table beside the Songo Lock of the Cumberland and Oxford Canal, a canal built in the 1830s, shortly after the Erie Canal, to haul timber from the lakes region to the sea. Today, the timber travels by truck and the lock is used only to lower small pleasure boats down to the lake from a nearby marina. It is operated entirely by hand. The park rangers push the lock gates open using only the leverage of a twenty-foot beam. It's quite a workout. They don't need any extra exercise in a gym at day's end.

After lunch, we pushed northward, weaving our way between the numerous small lakes that make this area so attractive. At every turn, the vistas through the trees took our breath away. When we saw the White Mountains in the distance as a backdrop, we were hooked. How great it would be to have a place here, something small, modest, an inexpensive cabin, to come and stay for a few weeks in the summer. We turned into the nearest real estate office, but when we saw the prices of the listings of the small modest "camps," we backed out the door as quickly as we had entered. "Oh well," as the fox in Aesop's fable so wisely said, "the grapes were probably sour." This place would be too cold in winter, and we probably wouldn't like it. Besides, we're boat people. Who would want to be stuck on the land? It's better for us to continue to enjoy the exquisite beauty of Maine from our boat sans our short lived dream of owning a cabin.

We drove on toward the White Mountains to Fryeburg where Gina and her husband Rick lived on a fifteen-acre farm. Gina raised perennial plants for the wholesale market, and Rick, a chef, who daily surprised and delighted two hundred elderly clients at the Senior Center with the gastronomical magic he created on a very frugal budget. Luke, their five-year-old, was so excited to have guests that he dressed up for the occasion with a tie, double-breasted coat, pants, white socks and boots...in ninety-five degree heat. Despite the electrical power being off most of the afternoon, Rick worked around that and concocted a gourmet meal, fit for visiting dignitaries. Gina showed us around her nursery and their one-hundred-year-old farmhouse which they have coaxed back to its former magnificence. They were gracious hosts. It was good to see them and to learn about their life in Maine first hand. Satiated with a fine dinner and with the shades of evening approaching, we drove back to Portland.

Our challenge was to find the Centerboard Yacht Club from the land, in the dark, using only a sketchy map. We had always approached the club from the water. We knew just where it was between other marinas and across from landmarks in the harbor. We could find it with ease by boat. How difficult could it be to find it from the land, by car? It wasn't that easy. It took several dead ends and as many "Oh! We've been here before just a few minutes ago." We finally located it, down at the end of the most unlikely street, the street which was so unlikely we'd driven past it at least three times. Sean, the launch driver, had remembered to leave a gate card in the mailbox for us so we could open the gate, get on to the dock, get in our dinghy, and get back to the boat. Thanks to him, we didn't have to sleep in the car. Our land adventure was a pleasant interlude to life on the water. We should do this kind of thing more often.

The next day was a lay-day, literally. We just lay around most of the day, as we planned to fly out the next day to Florida, to celebrate my sister's 50th wedding anniversary. We had several projects in mind, but initial inertia kicked in and we never made it beyond "initial." We did manage to pack clothes and prepare the boat for four days' absence. We secured everything on deck in case of a blow, doubled the mooring pennant, shut off the electric refrigerator, and closed off the through-hull valves.

Friday, we called the yacht club launch as soon as someone came on duty, requesting a ride across the harbor. We called for a taxi to pick us up, and sat on a log, waiting, at the front gate of DiMillo's Marina. A very long white limo drove up. The smiling driver got out and looked at us expectantly.

"You want to go to the airport?" he asked.

"Yes!" we sputtered, with an implied, You've got to be kidding. We had called a taxi, not a limo.

"I'm your taxi," he said, opening the door for us.

In the mornings when there's little demand for limos, they use them for ordinary taxi runs.

Scarcely able to control our mix of amusement, surprise, and incredulity, we climbed in the back seat of a stretch limo that was only slightly smaller than our 32' boat. It shattered all our images of limo mystique and our wonderings about the mysterious celebrities riding behind the smoked glass windows. Here we were, just plain Cliff and Bezy, and we were riding in a limo. We're certainly not celebrities nor are we mysterious. We were still laughing when we got out at the airport in shorts, T-shirts, and sandals, carrying our own bags. We disappeared into the terminal, chuckling at the thoughts of gaping bystanders trying to figure out who we were and why they didn't recognize us. It made our day! Yes, Russ, strange and wonderful things do happen to those of us who cruise. (Russ Fields is a cruising friend who is constantly surprised by the serendipities that happen.)

Continental Airlines whisked us to Florida for the celebration. We gave Anne and Berle a kite to inaugurate their "next 50 years" of married life. We hope it will help maintain the lilt in their step and the light heartedness in their lives. The anniversary party was held on a dinner cruise boat in Clearwater Bay, waters that I sailed many years ago. Today there are memories from childhood and loving time with family. Tonight I'll hurl through the sky. Then tomorrow I'll be on a boat in Maine ready for a summer of excitement and fun.

Chapter 4

To Boothbay

We flew back to Portland, intrigued by the contrast between the speed of modern day air travel versus our usual pace of 6 knots. We turned on the power, opened the through hulls and returned the boat to full operation. The refrigerator had defrosted, as expected, but its contents remained chilled by the cool nights and the cold sea water against the hull. Had we left the refrigerator on, it would have depleted the boat's batteries, leaving us literally dead in the water.

With our flying trip over, we were now ready to head further east, to our favorite parts of Maine. Portland is the western edge of the state's three large bays—Casco, Muscongus and Penobscot. We hope to get to Penobscot Bay and on beyond to Roque before the summer is over, and now it's time to begin our trek "down east." In Maine, when you sail to the Northeast, toward the farthest northern islands, it's called "down east." It is generally "east," and it's considered "down" because, with the prevailing westerly winds, you're sailing "down wind." Mainers have distinctive ways of expressing themselves, and if you want to communicate, it's important to "learn the language." Their speech is as rugged and distinctive as the Maine landscape.

Supplies are low, and Portland has the largest, best supplied grocery stores we'll see in a while. When we loaded our groceries and supplies in the cab, there was barely enough room for Bezy and me, but we didn't want the cab driver to drive away with our provisions unattended. We laughed when he asked us to provide directions back to the yacht club. He's local and he's supposed to know his way around. He lives and works here, but he couldn't find the Centerboard Club. We felt better about the difficulties we had had searching for it in the dark. We brought *Ceilidh* in to the dock to load the groceries, fill our water tanks, and top off the diesel fuel. We were finally ready to head "down east," well, at least seven miles, as far as Cliff Island.

The mark guiding us into the anchorage at Cliff Island was green. The chart showed it as red. The color indicates on which side to pass. Do we follow the buoy or the chart? As a compromise, we passed it close on our port, attempting to hedge our bets. We slowed to idle and crossed in water fifteen feet deep which was exactly what the chart showed it should be.

There was not enough space to anchor with adequate swinging room, but there were some unused moorings. We decided to poach one and silently thanked *Tortuga Escapade*, for the use of their mooring. It's general practice to "poach a mooring" and be prepared to move immediately if the owner shows up. This custom is another indication of both the practicality and the hospitality of Maine.

As the tide went out, two rock ledges were exposed on either side of us. The banks were marked in layers, the bottom layer was the dark brown kelp, next, a rust orange band, then a light tan one before the rock formation started breaking into squareish blocks, topped by a thin layer of grass and finally graceful spruce trees towered skyward. It is aesthetic surprises like these that give coastal Maine its unique character.

A sliver of moon eased toward the horizon just after sunset. There were only a couple of dots of light on the island. The dark of night was illumined by a brilliant starlit sky, stars spreading from horizon to horizon on a background of dark blue velvet. We sat in the cockpit drinking in the quiet and peace of the heavens. From time to time, a bird called in the distance. The wavelets lapped hesitantly on the rocks. The rest of the world was quiet and still. When we finally made our way to bed, I could still see the stars through the hatch over my berth. What a gift in this noisy artificially lit world. This is the lonely splendor of Maine.

We got underway next morning at a leisurely 7 o'clock, three hours after first light. It's hard to believe that daylight starts so early. We're at the eastern edge of the time zone, we're more than 43 degrees north of the equator, and it's only a couple of weeks after the summer solstice. All of these factors contribute to a very early sunrise this time of year.

We had an "oops!" with the engine, but it turned out to be only seaweed fouling the prop. Running a moment or two in reverse "unwound" the seaweed, and it floated away. Our diagnostic skills were a bit rusty so it took a few minutes of anxiousness to figure out what had happened, to confirm that the engine had no issues, to remember the corrective procedure, and to confirm that we were okay and didn't need to abort our plans for the day.

We were still getting used to navigating in and around rocks, getting accustomed to charts with lots of little circles on them indicating shallow spots, most of those spots being the peaks of rocks jutting up. Even in the midst of depth readings of 68,' 94,' or 110,' rocks can lie in wait just below the surface. Maine's unusual land formations require a different approach to navigation, and the fact that it's all rock raises the stakes considerably.

Today's passage to Boothbay took us out onto the open Atlantic off Casco Bay and further east to the entrance to Boothbay Harbor. The seas rolled in from the south, the air was cool and dry, and the wind gentle. The sails filled, and we made steady headway. We had only twenty-five nautical miles to go to Boothbay Harbor, a quaint, old steamship terminal and fishing harbor, one of the oldest in Maine. The weather had settled and there were no storms in the forecast. We passed several other sailboats underway, a first for the season. It looks like summer has finally arrived, and other boaters have arrived as well.

As we rounded Tumbler Island ledge and entered Boothbay Harbor, we were overtaken by *Eastwinds* as it glided easily past, making effective use of the light winds. When we landed, we went over to where they were docked and visited with them. *Eastwinds* is a replica of the classic Maine fishing schooner, newly built, light and modern. She is surprisingly fast. Her owners, who are also her captain and crew, built the boat themselves five years ago to take passengers on harbor cruises. They offer three cruises each day, enough for them to make a living doing what they love.

In addition to *Eastwinds*'s, several traditional windjammers sail out of Boothbay. These are old boats, not modern replicas, former working schooners modified to take passengers for a week's sail. The passengers help raise the sails and hoist the anchor to the rhythms of the old sea shanties just like a century ago. They eat much better than the fishermen, and they don't work nearly as hard. It's difficult to imagine a better week's vacation than such a cruise and the experience it offers.

Boothbay Harbor is filled with moorings and lobster pots. It takes all eyes available to track them so you don't catch them on the rudder or keel. There is a vast array of boats moving about in a very congested area, especially a number of lobstermen tending their traps. The small harbor is further reduced in size by the buildings, restaurants and inns that are built out over the water, encroaching on the already diminished space. Working boatmen seem to recognize the value of the tourists and make a real effort to coexist, despite the antics of pleasure craft and the crowding of their work area. Later in the summer, when the sea water warms, the lobster will move out of the harbor into cooler deeper water, and the lobstermen will no longer have to fish in the harbor, but for now, it's crowded and quite a challenge to everyone, especially to a visiting captain.

Ashore, there are a variety of shops and other attractions that would evoke a smile from P.T. Barnum. Boothbay has a reputation as a tourist haven, and after all, we are tourists. Our two favorite shops are the Shirt Shop that has T-shirts for $5 and sweatshirts for $10, emblazoned with local logos and sayings. My favorite is "Maine, the way life should be." I have a number of message T-shirts that never evoke a response, but whenever I wear this one from Maine, invariably I'm asked, "Are you from Maine?"

I answer, a little embarrassed, "No, but I've been there...and it's a wonderful place...and I'm looking forward to returning."

After I'd answered in that manner, one man informed me,

"If someone asks if you're from Maine, there's only one right answer."

"What's that?" I asked, interestedly.

"Ayuh," he replied.

My other favorite shop is the Ice Cream Factory where a "make it yourself" banana split was almost...emphasis on "almost"... more than I could manage. It took a couple of brief pauses, but finally, I was able to empty the bowl. I was on to them the next time I was there. I by-passed the do-it-yourself servings, and ordered four scoops. They surprised me with a sizable vegetable dish filled with more than a pint of mint chocolate chip ice cream. I normally avoid ice cream sold by the scoop since many times I've been served a small dollop that only pretended to be a scoop. The Ice Cream Factory is serious about ice cream and is committed to the fact that no one leaves without generous servings. I don't know whether it's on "The Maine Ice Cream Trail," but if it isn't, it certainly should be. Now that's my kind of trail.

There are many things to do in Boothbay Harbor besides a schooner ride, buying t-shirts, and eating ice cream. You can buy a lobster at the lobster pound. They'll cook it for you and send you back to eat it on your boat complete with corn on the cob and slaw. Curio and small gift shops abound as do a wide variety of eateries. You can't go hungry if you try, whether you arrived here from the land or the sea.

We took a mooring with the Tug Boat Inn. The mooring was so close to the inn that the guests looked down into our cockpit from their balconies. We were so close that we could push off from the boat and make it to the dock in an inflatable dinghy without rowing a single stroke. The noises of the busy harbor, land traffic, and people talking and laughing were in stark contrast to the quiet of the previous night when we heard only the sea lapping against the rock and the call of the gulls.

Chapter 5

Muscongus Bay and Morse Island

In the morning we were ready to move on. There were two possibilities for the day. We could go directly to Morse Island in Muscongus Bay to visit our friends Dick and Jean Killough. Or we could round Pemaquid Point and head east, out into the open Atlantic to Monhegan Island. If we go to Monhegan, we'd spend several hours there, and then make our way to Morse just before dark.

Monhegan is a remote fishing village where a colony of artists, inspired by its sea swept isolation, live in concert with the fishermen. Its moorings are owned by the fishing fleet and anchoring is very demanding. The harbor is exposed to south winds and swells. You take your boat there with fear and trepidation. We decided to wait until we get outside on the ocean and know the wind and sea conditions before we made our decision as to which place to go.

Monhegan Harbor

After a breakfast ashore of finnian haddie, creamed haddock on toast, we dropped the mooring pennant and began to pick our way carefully between mooring buoys and lobster pots. As we tried to dodge a small lobster boat working his pots, *Ceilidh* crunched her keel on the rocks. With only 3 knots of speed, it was disconcerting but not damaging to the boat, only to the captain's self image and spirits. Our keel is very stout. It is molded as an integral part of the hull, not just bolted on. We scrunched a second time, and then we were clear. Looking back, we were well within the mooring field when we hit. I assumed a mooring field would have a minimum depth of 5' but obviously my assumption was wrong. There were more dangers lurking beneath the surface than met the eye. I quickly upgraded my attention level as we continued out of the harbor. When we finally cleared the outer marks, and it was no longer congested, I resumed breathing.

We left Squirrel Island on our starboard, passing between Linekin Neck and Fisherman Island, turned east past Thrumcap and went on to Pemaquid Point. By now we had passed the last of the islands that shelter the entrance to Boothbay and were fully exposed to the open ocean with its long running swells of 6' to 7'. The ridges of rock formed by glaciers from the ice age that reach out into the Atlantic provide a puzzling mix of protection from the ocean winds and swells. It takes lots of experience to predict where one can expect protection, and where one is exposed. The weather forecast called for 15 knots from the south, but as usual it was understated. Several stations were already reporting 20 knots. Today is not a good day to go to Monhegan. The swells on our beam would give us an uncomfortable roll on the passage across, and the anchoring, exposed to the south, would be highly questionable for even a short time.

So we bore off to the northwest past West Egg Rock for a more comfortable ride. We had heard they are attempting to reestablish a colony of puffins on nearby East Egg Island, and although we searched for them as we passed close to East Egg, we were disappointed not to see any of these unusual looking birds nesting among the rocks. We continued on to Morse Island to visit our friends Jean and Dick Killough at their summer place. Jean's grandfather bought land here for the timber. After harvesting the trees, he sold off all the land except for a lot for a house. Dick and I both taught at Drury College in Springfield, Missouri in the

1970s, and he and his family has spent their summers here for the past 54 years.

Morse is right next to Friendship Island, the center of Maine's lobster industry. It is not surprising that here the lobster floats are so numerous and very close together. They're so close that they look like multicolored sprinkles on a sugar cookie. We wove our way through them like a shuttle threading a loom. The only good news is that they were brightly colored with an attached stick that stands up making them more visible than the stone crab and blue crab traps we're accustomed to dodging in Florida and in the Chesapeake. Those floats are smaller and much harder to see. We were concentrating so hard on avoiding the lobster floats that we lost our bearings and wound up in a different channel, one island over from Morse. The island sequence wasn't like the chart, nor were the channel marks in their expected places. We asked a lobsterman running traps nearby, and he identified the islands, reorienting us. We were soon back on track.

Morse is small, a little more than a mile in diameter, with a thick stand of spruce trees leading down to a rocky shore. The rocks were covered with kelp and other sea weed at low tide. We found the cove on the northeast corner that Dick had mentioned and dropped the hook. I dinghied ashore and inquired about the Killoughs. It's a small place so everyone knows everyone's comings and goings. "The Killoughs arrived about an hour ago," the neighbor said. He asked his son Keith, age seven, to walk with me to their house. Keith introduced us to each family along the way, but that was not necessary. They already knew who we were and that we had arrived. News travels very fast on a small Maine island. They had nice comments to make about our boat; they had already seen it anchored in the cove. Mike, the handyman, who works on many of the island's houses, greeted us, "So good to see you again. Dick told me you were coming. How's the sailing?"

Morse Island's claim to fame is as one of the first places where the famous Friendship Sloops were built. Wilbur Morse was one of the principle builders. These graceful sloops were handled by a single fisherman and fished these waters around the turn of the

20th century. They were designed and built when the fishing industry moved inshore and smaller boats were needed to fish the shallower waters near the land.

Morse boatshed on Morse Island
Photo courtesy Friendship Sloop Society

The house Jean inherited was built by her grandfather in the 1840s. Some of the original, rough-hewn beams were still visible, a reminder of its age. It's located on an island, so the electricity is battery powered, and recharged by solar panels. Dick and his sons were building a post and beam addition that will provide three additional bedrooms so the whole family can stay here at the same time. They've added a composting toilet and running water, pumping it from a nearby well, which they once used when they brought water to the house in buckets and pails. They have also added refrigeration and heating, thanks to propane gas. And in case modern conveniences break down, the old outhouse, just down the path, remains with its charming Dutch doors so you can have a little privacy while at the same time enjoying the view.

The Killoughs are as charming as their house. Dick is the consummate pastor and professor with a genuine care for everyone he meets. Jean is a mother who tends to her flock and provides for family and friends with good food and much care and attention. We caught up on what had happened in their family and shared memories of the good times we had had in Springfield, Missouri. We spent the nights on the boat, but spent the days on the island, exploring, visiting and renewing friendships both with the Killoughs and with everyone else on the island who still remembered us from four years ago.

The wildlife didn't seem very wild. A small red fox walked past the window with no concern for the people around. Red squirrels scampered up the trees and peeked around at us from the back side. Two very young raccoons stood and watched on the path as we passed. As I stooped to take a picture, one moved toward me with a questioning look, as if asking "Are you my mama?" This is unusual behavior for wild animals, but obviously these are not very wild and have become accustomed to the non-threatening people with whom they live.

The Killoughs' daughter Ruthie and her family were there as well. Ruthie's husband Bill and their five-year-old son Charlie took us on a walk down to the south shore beach, passing through "the forest primeval," a stand of spruce trees in a swampy area. The trees were so thick they blocked out the sun. The ground was carpeted with moss in variegated greens, interspersed with fern and spruce cones. The still air, damp, moist, and devoid of direct sunlight, was a favorite breeding place for mosquitoes. As we approached, one of them shouted, "Fresh blood!" and they mounted a full scale attack.

After two-thirds of a mile, the path opened on to the island's south beach, a rock-strewn, kelp-covered slope at the water's edge. Small wavelets lapped lazily against the rocks. The fog that had teased all day now settled in. It was impossible to see beyond the small waves toppling up on the shore. The limbs of a downed weathered gray tree close to the water's edge provided a prop for pictures of Charlie. He perched on the trunk, swung from a branch and peeked from underneath. Returning through the trees and once again the gauntlet of mosquitoes, we discovered we fared better if we kept moving, moving fast, better still, running.

The next day we took our hosts for a sail to nearby Otter Island. The wind was light and it wasn't much of a sail, more a slat

where the sails hang limp and the gentle swells flop them about
with not enough wind to hold them in place. Around 11:30, the
haze burned off, the wind freshened, and we could sail. When we
returned to Morse, the tide was high. We took *Ceilidh* in to the
landing float and put our passengers off on the dock. This
morning, at low tide, there wasn't a foot of water at the float. So
much for Maine's nine-foot tides.

Dick and I took his runabout and went over to the lobster
wharfs at Friendship to buy some lobsters for dinner. Dick chose
shedders. Locals prefer the shedders because lobsters are more
tender right after they have shed their former shell than later when
they have filled it out again. We put our eight shedders in the family
lobster box, floating in the water alongside the dock. This way the
lobsters could remain in sea water until we were ready to cook
them. Earlier, we had put two pots of sea water out in the sun to
warm while we sailed. Jean, like all good Maine cooks, cooks
lobster in sea water for better flavor. Jean said, "I'm so grateful you
know how to eat lobster, and I can bypass the usual instructional
session on breaking claws to dig out the meat and how to suck the
goodies out of the legs." We donned our bibs, took up our pliers
and picks and dug in. They were tender and delicious, accompanied
by fresh-baked blueberry muffins, and raspberries that Charlie had
picked especially for us earlier that afternoon.

After dinner, we gathered with most of the other islanders at
the oldest home on the island, the house of a granddaughter of
Wilbur Morse. She pointed to the third floor loft over the codfish
drying sheds where Wilbur built his boats. The difficulty of getting
the sloops to the water was less important than having an enclosed
place to work, away from the cold winter winds. You could always
rig up some sort of tackle and a horse drawn cart to move the boat
to the water from even a third floor loft. The gathering was a brief
celebration of the Fourth of July. We had punch and cookies and
lots of conversation.

A third generation islander whom we met four years ago, was
a Coast Guard pilot, currently stationed in Elizabeth City, North
Carolina. As we talked with him about his work, he mentioned a

rescue mission he flew over Albermarle Sound earlier that spring, about the time we were trying to cross the sound. "We remember that mission," we said. "We listened to what was happening on *Ceilidh*'s VHF radio. A 40' cruiser was taking on water in 35 knots of wind and steep high seas."

The Albemarle is a large body of shallow water that is notorious and dangerous. Water was rising rapidly in the boat. While her husband was working desperately to save their boat, his wife was communicating with the Coast Guard by radio. She was very frightened; you could hear the fear in her voice. The plane dropped an emergency pump to help them dewater the boat. About that time, the Coast Guard shifted to another VHF channel, and we didn't hear the final outcome.

The pilot said, "I can complete the story. We circled for awhile until we could tell the pump was removing the water. We were low on fuel and had to return to our base. They were on their own all night, but we sent out a boat to tow them in the next morning. The couple made it back to the land and the boat was saved."

We heard this event on our radio while anchored less than eight miles away in the shelter of an island, safe and secure. The weather was so bad throughout the whole area that a Coast Guard helicopter flew in low above us at our anchorage and hailed us on the radio to make sure we were alright. We were riding comfortably on our anchor in the lee of the island, reading, checking the weather forecasts and listening to PBS on the radio. We appreciated the Coast Guard's concern. It's nice to know they're there if you need them. Thus far, we've not had to call on them for help.

After a pleasant evening with the Killoughs' neighbors on Morse Island, we returned to *Ceilidh*, just before dark. The fog was so thick, we were barely able to make out her outline from the dock only 15 yards away. We pushed off in the dinghy trying to maintain a precise course. We managed to make the few yards safely. I'm not sure what we'd have done had we missed our boat other than muddle around until we hit something, the boat, the dock, or the shore. The cove wasn't that big.

It was the Fourth of July, but we didn't expect fireworks in this remote area. To our surprise some of the neighbors exploded a few rockets, at least that's what we thought happened. It sounded more like a thud or thump than the crack of fireworks. The fog changes everything, both sights and sounds. We went up on deck to look around but we saw nothing, nothing but the misty gray fog packed in tight around us. I don't remember any Fourth of July quite like it.

Next morning, Ruthie, Bill and the boys had to leave for home. Dick and I loaded them into Dick's 16' runabout and took them to their car which they'd left parked in Friendship. We also wanted to buy more lobster for supper. Dick introduced me to several lobstermen he's known through the years as we asked around the docks for someone who had lobster to sell. I'd just finished reading *The Lobster Harbor Gangs*, a study of lobster fishing and the social organization of how it's done and who's allowed to fish. It's hard, really impossible, for those "from away" to break into the close knit units. Fishing is reserved for the men of the village, their sons and others who are born here, though increasingly women are beginning to fish and captain their own boats and are included. Each harbor has a territory for its traps which they protect from encroachment with whatever it takes. The old wooden traps are no longer used except to sell to tourists for porch or garden decorations. Modern traps are made of vinyl-covered wire, four feet long and with an escape door for small lobsters. They have a larger biodegradable port that opens in case the trap gets lost. This way the lobster can escape and not die needlessly in an abandoned trap.

Shake shingle siding

Despite the fact that Dick has been coming here every summer for 54 years, he is still "from away," not "from here." Jean's father owned Morse Island, yet that does not qualify her as "from here." Had she been born on the island and lived here all her life, that would make her "from here." Only those who leave for military service and return can maintain their status as "from here." This is the first time we encountered this important distinction; no doubt we'll run into it again.

As we moved about the harbor, Dick spotted a friend who had just launched his new boat and was filling it with gas.

"What a fine-looking boat. Are you happy with it?"

"Ayuh." Pete replied.

"Does it handle well?"

"Ayuh."

"Are you using gasoline?" Dick asked in surprise when he noted the fuel he was pumping into his tank was not diesel.

"Ayuh," was the terse but complete answer.

"Why didn't you get a Diesel?" asked Dick.

"Stupid," said Pete.

Conversations with a Mainer are short, candid, to the point and sometimes painfully truthful.

The sunlight gave way to the soft glow of gas lights as we finished fresh lobster, expertly prepared in a simple setting with close friends. This straightforward, plain style of life is what Maine is all about. It's easy to understand what has brought Dick and Jean back here every summer even though they live and work two thousand miles away on the far side of Missouri.

Chapter 6

Audubon Camp and Muscongus Bay

Next morning as we pulled the anchor, our wash-down pump that's used to clean the mud off the anchor and chain didn't work. Plan B! We pulled out the brush that fits around the chain, hooked it with the boat hook, and worked it up and down to clear the mud.

We sailed through Friendship Harbor, in one side and out the other, into Muscongus Bay, up the east side of Bremen Long Island, around the northern point and down the west side, just enjoying the sights and the aroma of the conifers on the islands nearby. One of the joys of sailing in Maine is the aroma of the trees and their pungent fragrance as it drifts out across the water. First time visitors to these shores knew they were approaching land by the pungent smell of trees before they could see land over the horizon. The early morning sun was at just the right angle to highlight the different shapes of the trees, bringing out their full texture as well as the shadows and highlights. We had not remembered that green came in so many tints and hues.

We passed the north tip of Hog Island, the location of the Audubon Society's camp, on our way to anchor in Greenland Cove. A few houses were visible along the banks with docks and boats interrupting the shore line; otherwise it appeared to be a forested paradise. The tall straight spruce trees with turned up branches blanketed the islands right down to the rocky shore. The lobstermen worked their boats close up against the rocks where they'd laid their traps. The gulls hovered noisily overhead, hoping for a handout.

As we anchored, two women, with an accompanying rowboat, swam across the cove passing near us. Noting our hailing port of St. Petersburg, Florida, they took time to welcome us to Maine. They also invited us to join them as they swam. The water was clear and inviting, but before we jumped in we reminded ourselves how cold it was and decided to enjoy its crystal brilliance from a distance. A red-hulled sloop with classic lines was moored near the shore.

It was warm enough to sit out in the cockpit and enjoy the day, one of the first warm days we've encountered thus far. There were several boat projects to do, but they'll have to wait. We've gotten good this summer at putting off work. We got out our reading and kicked back. Coots floated on the water, then they'd sort of jump up and dive under in search of fish. We heard a few loons, but it was not until after dark, when we'd settled into bed that they captured the night, calling to each other across the cove with their haunting "Hoo hoo! Hoo hoo!"

Next day, the lobstermen were out at dawn, working their traps. They'd run one line of traps and then go full speed to the next set, only 50 yards away, starting and stopping, creating a significant wake. There were several boats out, and each boat was working multiple sets of traps. After being jostled by the wakes for awhile, we were thoroughly awake, so we concluded it was time to get up and enjoy the day. We began with breakfast in the cockpit, something we hadn't been able to do in a long time. A leisurely cup of coffee, hot cereal, fruit and toast is simple fare, but the setting, at anchor, in a cove, in Maine, with a panorama of trees along the shore, makes it a feast for a king.

When we dinghied over to the Audubon camp, we encountered a group of artists who were there for the week, sketching birds and painting the island scenes. Another group of campers were on a kayak adventure, kayaking around the island and venturing out into the nearby waters. The Audubon Society offers a variety of programs that groups and individuals can enjoy in this isolated setting.

We walked one of the trails in search of an eagle's nest. The tall straight spruce trees with their stubby, short, dead branches at the lower levels were not quite as dense as the grove on Morse Island. Here, sunlight sprinkled down, occasionally reaching the carpet of needles and cones that made up the ground cover. The trees' roots formed a mosaic across the top of the ground. Wild flowers and green moss were interspersed with small spots of sunlight on the forest floor. An occasional view of the rocky shoreline could be seen through the trees. It was a pleasant walk, but we didn't spot any eagles. The thick mat of branches overhead made it difficult to see the treetops where eagles nest. The walk through the forest, however, was a nice change for boat-bound cruisers. We admired the paintings of the budding artists as we passed each easel. Then we thanked our hosts at the camp and headed back to the dock where our dinghy was tied.

As we were about to push away from the dock, an approaching boat hailed us. To our surprise, we heard: "Bezy? Cliff?" John and Connie Towne who live across the bay were taking Connie's mother for a ride. They had spotted *Ceilidh* at anchor with its dinghy missing and surmised we were at the Audubon camp. We had communicated by e-mail that we were coming, and they offered us use of their mooring in front of their camp. (Camp is a Maine term for a house on the water with traditional Maine understatement. Nowhere else would such beautiful houses be called camps.) They gave us instructions on how to identify their mooring. We returned to *Ceilidh*, up anchored, motored a mile-and-a-half to Muscongus Harbor and picked up the mooring.

Ceilidh at anchor

We met John and Connie in Marsh Harbor, in the Bahamas several years ago and have kept in touch. John had marked the good anchorages for us on our Maine charts, based on his extensive experience sailing and cruising here. We've tried out a number of the anchorages and are grateful to him for sharing his knowledge. Sharing local knowledge is a common practice among cruisers. One who knows an area will mark the charts for a newcomer who's headed that way.

So much has happened since we were together that the conversation was nonstop through a steak-on-the-grill dinner, finished with, ice cream, of course. All my friends know my passion for ice cream.

John had just returned from sailing a friend's boat back from Bermuda to Marion, Massachusetts. The 30-knot winds made for a fast but demanding trip. Earlier this summer, he raced to Halifax, Nova Scotia in fog "so thick you couldn't see the bow." In that race, a fellow competitor hit a fishing boat while flying along in thick fog with a spinnaker set. The friend tried to report the accident to the Coast Guard, but their radio was too weak. John's boat offered to relay the message. When they heard the friend's position, they realized to their horror that they were in the exact same place, and they too were surfing with their spinnaker flying. They doubled their bow watch and their prayers as they relayed the message. They never saw or heard either of the boats involved in the accident.

John serves as a volunteer for the Maine Kayak Trail Society and makes frequent trips to several nearby islands which he monitors to make sure visitors are using them appropriately. The Kayak Trail covers much of coastal Maine, allowing one to paddle from island to island, camping ashore overnight.

Connie and John had to return to their home in Winslow for the day to tend to some business. While they were gone, we read, used our computer with unlimited electrical power, and enjoyed a hot shower, all great luxuries for those of us who live on boats. It's just as well we were ashore, since *Ceilidh* was socked in in the fog the entire day. It lifted, sort of, for a couple of hours in early afternoon but quickly returned. It felt good to just stay put. In the afternoon, we gathered mussels from the nearby rocks, put them in a bucket of fresh water so they could clean themselves of sand, and, at dinner time, cooked them in white wine.

The next morning, John called over to us on board *Ceilidh*. "The mackerel are running. Let's go fishing." We set out in their power boat to fish in the channel east of Pemaquid Point. I've never fished with such continuous activity and excitement. We trolled two lines with several triple barbed hooks on each line. We fished without a smidgen of bait, only the bare silver hooks. But as soon as the line was out, we pulled it back with a fish on every hook, eight to ten mackerel each time. The fish didn't seem to notice the lack of bait. They struck the flashing silver of the hook. In less than ten minutes we had all the mackerel we could use and headed home. I'm not much of a fisherman but when the fish are biting like that, that's my kind of fishing.

Chapter 7

To Port Clyde and on to Monhegan Island

We still wanted to go to Monhegan. But after our aborted attempt to sail there a few days back, we decided to take the mail boat that leaves daily from Port Clyde instead of attempting to go there aboard *Ceilidh*. We'll sail over to Port Clyde on the St. George River, take a mooring in the fishing village, and arrange for tomorrow morning's departure on the boat to Monhegan.

John said, "On your way to Port Clyde, you should stop by Round Pond, a couple of miles south of Muscongus Harbor, and check out a 65' blue-hulled sailboat moored there. She is a beauty with sleek lines, shining teak and a graceful, nicely balanced rig." As we drew alongside the yacht, we circled slowly, trying to control our exclamations of awe and amazement. She was as pretty a vessel as the place she was anchored. Round Pond is a great natural harbor on the east side of the Pemaquid Peninsula, a home for both working boats and pleasure craft. The kids were out racing in a wooden knockabout design that I was not familiar with. There are a number of local one-design classes in New England. A group of yacht clubs in a given area selected a design and all the clubs built fleets of the same boat. It makes for great competitive racing. Although the sailing season is limited, they make the most of it here in Maine and get in lots of sailing in the brief summer months.

Leaving Round Pond, we could either retrace our steps around the north tip of Hog Island and the Audubon Camp, or we could cross the submerged ledge south of the island, saving several miles. The submerged ledge is known as the Hog Island Bar. It is actually an underwater continuation of the island itself. The chart showed rocks and other "bad" things that "go bump on the bottom of boats," but John assured us there was a safe channel at this tide. He had sailed these waters for many years and was quite knowledgeable. We spotted the local "white stake," a three-inch

PVC pipe pounded down into the bottom marking the deepest water. We hugged it close, like it was Mama's skirt, and passed in nine feet of water, more than enough for *Ceilidh*'s four-and-a-half foot draft.

Beyond the bar we turned northeast and again passed through Friendship harbor and around Morse Island. Once again, we negotiated the densest collection of lobster pots we've come across. It was a major challenge to find a path wide enough for our boat's ten-feet-three-inch beam to squeeze between the floats. As we struggled to avoid them and recalled the consequences of snagging one...especially diving in the frigid water...we repeated over and over, "We love to eat lobster. We love to eat lobster. We love to eat lobster."

Passing south of Gay Island, we reached the St. George River and headed up toward Hubble Island opposite Port Clyde. I hailed Dick and Suzi on the VHF radio, long time cruising friends who were planning to be in this area today. We hoped they were already in radio range, and to our delight they were. They were about 13 miles behind us, headed up the river to Thomaston to visit friends who live there. We made plans to join them several days from now in Rockland.

We rounded Hubble Island and entered Port Clyde from the south. I called the harbor master on Channel 16. He directed me to an available mooring, one of the cone shaped ones that belonged to the General Store, a truly old fashioned general store that has survived the changes of time by continuing to serve the village's needs. We bought tickets for tomorrow's boat to Monhegan, walked the town...in about seven minutes...and enjoyed an impromptu "Tour de Port Clyde" bike race by the local eleven-year-olds, down the hill, around the old tree, a short cut across a vacant lot, ending with a slide out in front of the local ice cream shop. We bought a few groceries and dinghied back to the boat.

To our surprise, in the hour we'd been gone, the mooring field had quickly filled with transient boats, the most transient boats we've seen thus far. One couple from a trimaran struggled to start their 5 horse power Mercury on their dinghy. They were drifting

Moored boats at Port Clyde

slowly in the direction they wanted to go as he pulled...and pulled...and pulled on the starter cord. The motor gave not a single cough. I offered sympathy and encouragement but decided not to mention that I had been sorely tempted to convert a similar 5 hp Mercury into an anchor after a lot of time and money invested vainly encouraging it to start and run...to no avail. Mercury confirmed that that model had a serious problem when they discontinued it after only six months production.

As the sun fell below the horizon, we sat in the cockpit, sipping wine and nibbling munchies. But our reverie was disturbed by a surprising wave action that jostled us late into the evening. There was no plausible explanation as to what caused it. We ruled out both wakes from boats and swells coming in from the sea as its source. It was puzzling!

We dinghied over to the town dock the next morning and boarded the *Elizabeth Anne* along with one hundred and thirty of our newest friends for the 10:30 trip to Monhegan Island. Before we left, they cautioned us to take all the water we needed for the day. "Plan to use the heads on the boat, but don't expect to use any restrooms on the island. They have a severe water crisis. A water line burst, and until it's fixed, they have to import all their water."

It was a bright sunny day, just the right weather for an excursion to a windswept island out in the ocean...with or without water.

As we passed between Allen and Burnt Islands, owned by members of the Wyeth family, the boat slowed so we could get a good look at the seals...harp, spotted and gray...sunning themselves on the dry ledges. There were about thirty seals and pups enjoying the warm rocks just above the water's edge. Their brown coats look so much like the color of the rocks that I missed them at first, mistaking them for just a few more rocks. But when the rocks moved, they popped into focus as seals.

A little later, the captain slowed again and pointed out a 40' minke whale to starboard. It rolled three times about a hundred yards off. On the third roll, it arched its back and dove deep. A deep dive usually lasts for several minutes so we moved on, deciding not to wait for another view.

In less than an hour, we pulled into the wharf of Monhegan Island, a stand-alone rock only a mile by a half mile in size. This sentinel, out in the Atlantic, is home to fishermen and artists, a strange and wonderful combination, who share a love for Monhegan because of its unique rugged beauty or its close proximity to the bounty of the ocean. Monhegan was visited by some of the first Europeans who came to this country. They came here then for the same reasons as now, to fish and explore. And before the Europeans, native Americans lived here, evidenced by their flint points found in the soil. A determined colony of fishermen has earned a living from its fecund waters for centuries. More than a hundred years ago, artists found their inspiration from its distinctive light and vistas and came here and joined the fishermen.

Artist at Monhegan

Today belonged to the artists. There were artists on the beach, on the rocks, in the town, in the fields, and on the porch of the hotel...painting. By contrast we saw no lobstermen. There were a half dozen lobster boats on moorings, but none out fishing. Lobster traps weren't in the water; they were stacked in rows all over the island, with weeds growing up through them. A mound

Monhegan lobster traps

of line lay in a neat coil beside each trap. We were told they fish only between December 1st and May 31st on Monhegan.

But the artists...ah, the artists! They were everywhere. There were resident artists and visiting artists, professional artists and student artists. On the beach, artists stood at their easels painting. In the town, artists were capturing this weathered building or that. On the trails, artists were looking for new inspiration. There were art classes for newcomers. There was an art show on the porch of the Monhegan Inn. Some painters, we were told, get together with their friends and come here every year for a week or two. Several noted artists have painted here, such as, Andrew and Jamie Wyeth, Edward Hopper, and Rockwell Kent. It's a seemingly congenial mix of Maine fishermen and artists.

Today the island thrives on the tourists who come to paint, or to watch those who do. Locals sell food, drinks, trinkets and anything else people will buy. The *Elizabeth Anne* and the *Laura S*, the two boats of the Monhegan Boat Line, bring everything to the island that arrives here...people, luggage, food stuffs, and freight. With the water shortage, our boat brought two fifty-five gallon drums of water "to flush the toilets." As we waited at the dock for our return trip, the *Laura S* arrived and unloaded extensive food supplies to be served in the inns and the hotel. There were also four huge baskets of laundry with sheets and towels. With the water shortage, the hotel returned these to the mainland for washing, and the boat brought them back cleaned.

There's going to be a wedding on Monhegan tomorrow. We watched the bride and groom welcome family for the big occasion. Grandma was helped off the boat in her wheel chair, assured the golf cart was nearby, ready to transport her to the hotel. The groom asked the boat's captain about the tables...and the flowers. They were expected to be on this trip. "We didn't have room on the 3:00 trip to bring either the tables or the flowers, water was deemed more urgent," the Captain explained, "the tables and flowers will be on the boat first thing tomorrow."

Our cruising guide discouraged cruisers coming to Monhegan because of the lack of moorings and the poor holding on the kelp covered rock. We asked locals about the situation and were directed to Sherman, a lobsterman who was selling seafood off Fish Beach. He assured us that moorings were available for $15 per night and wondered where the cruising guides got their misinformation. "Lobstermen rent their moorings during the summer when they are not fishing and their lobster boats are stored on the land," he said. Looking out over the harbor, I counted at least a dozen unoccupied moorings. "Anchoring," he said, "is not recommended because of the poor holding. The bottom is mostly rock, and there's kelp, large heavy sea weed, that will foul an anchor and keep it from catching. Nor is the somewhat exposed harbor comfortable in bad weather, either at anchor or on a mooring. But on reasonable days, the welcome mat is out, and moorings are readily available. Bring your boat and come!"

Monhegan lobster boats

We bought two of Sherman's lobster rolls and slaw for our lunch. For dessert, we found The Novelty which served ice cream. We tried their lemon sherbet. Its tangy taste was so extraordinary that Bezy insisted on seconds which was quite a switch as I'm usually the one having seconds of ice cream.

The highlight of our visit to Monhegan was the climb to the lighthouse and its accompanying Island Museum that displays artifacts of the island's history. The museum, housed in the former lighthouse keeper's quarters, included a display of antique fishing gear and a fully equipped kitchen from the turn of the century. It was a bit scary when the museum kitchen had all the utensils I remembered from my childhood home growing up. Maybe I am older than I thought. The lighthouse had a panoramic view

overlooking the harbor and the distant islands as far off as Mount
Desert. A cool breeze felt like air conditioning as we sat on benches
near the top of the island, resting and drinking in this windblown
wonder.

Bezy found some sea glass, tossed and rounded by the water's
constant motion hitting it against the rocks. She took it to an island
jeweler who glued on caps to make earrings. A tired but happy pair
of travelers boarded the boat for the homeward trip as the sun
eased down toward the horizon.

On the boat, we chatted with a couple from Georgia who were
in Maine as part of an Airstream International Rally. They were
headed to Nova Scotia. We shared some of our adventures in Nova
Scotia a few years back, including the tale about the bees,
transported on a semi-tractor trailer that moved up the east coast,
pollinating the citrus crop in Florida, then the peaches in Georgia
and South Carolina, next the apples in Virginia, pears and cherries
in New England, and finally the blueberries in Nova Scotia...all the
while, living in their hives on a truck that moved to a different place
each night. As our friends were chuckling at this unusual bit of
trivia, a man nearby who had overheard our story chimed in,
"That's true! I drive one of those trucks." He was from
Englewood, Florida, not far from where we live in Fort Myers.

We picked up a pizza at the General Store on the way back to
the boat. The moorings had emptied and refilled during the day so
we had all new neighbors for the evening. The mysterious rocking
of the night before was gone, although the currents and the wind
direction was the same as last night. It was still puzzling.

Chapter 8

Tenant's Harbor and a major Serendipity

Today the forecast calls for rain and a front to come through, but to our surprise the wind is in the east. You expect a front to approach either from the north or the southwest, but not from the east. I didn't understand the weather.

According to the cruising guide, there is a laundry, a chandlery, a small grocery store, moorings and good food available in Tenants Harbor on the other side of the peninsula from Port Clyde only seven miles away. We dropped our mooring pennant and headed there.

Out in the open, the wind gusted to 22 knots, on our nose, of course. The two to three-foot swells pulled the lobster pots underwater, making them difficult to see and a challenge to track. It required close attention, very close attention, to miss each and every one. We passed Mosquito Island, Mosquito Harbor and Mosquito Head. Russ, a cruising friend and guru, cautioned us years ago to pay close attention to the names of places...Cape Fear...Cape of Storms...Hell Gate...Mosquito Lagoon and the like. "Those names are not assigned casually, those places have *earned* their names. Pay attention and learn!" We decided to by-pass this area associated with mosquitoes and move on up the coast. We rounded Southern Island, a place you'll recognize in some of Andrew Wyeth's paintings, and turned in towards Tenants Harbor.

The harbor is exposed to the east, so unless the wind dies, it will be a bouncy night. The rain is holding off, at least for now, but the clouds look dark and threatening. It might not hold off very long.

We picked up a mooring for Cod End, a combined restaurant, dock, and marina that was noted for excellent seafood and blueberry pie at reasonable prices. Bezy organized the laundry as the rain clouds drew closer, darkening the sky. We gathered the trash and three boat bags of dirty clothes and loaded them in the dinghy just as it started to rain. At the town dock, we pushed the other dinghies apart and squeezed *Wee Ceilidh* in, at least close enough to get off on the dock. Gathering our boat bags, we walked over to Cod End to pay the mooring fee.

When we asked directions to the laundromat, we were told it closed a couple of months ago to make room for a new restaurant. The grocery store was still there, but it was small with only a limited supply of fresh vegetables, and vegetables were what we needed. That left only the post office and the chandlery on our "to do" list.

Leaving our clothes in a corner in the empty restaurant, we walked two blocks to the post office. The chute for out-of-town mail had printed underneath it "away." Mainers, like the Greeks, divide the known world into two groups. In ancient Greece you were either Greek or barbarian. In Maine you're either "from here" or "from away." We're clearly "from away." We asked the post mistress if she had a package for us in General Delivery. We had given this address to receive a couple of vital boat parts. Nothing had arrived. We had seen the chandlery from the water, so we asked directions from the post mistress. "It is closed. It hasn't opened yet for the season," she said. "But," she offered, "there is a parade tomorrow at ten o'clock, celebrating the town's bicentennial." A parade is always nice, but at the moment, a parade didn't seem a fair substitute for either badly needed boat parts or clean clothes, or the opportunity to buy vegetables and fruit. In addition, it had begun to rain hard, a serious "frog strangling" rain.

As we walked back to the Cod End in a soaking rain, we were wet through and through despite our waterproof rain gear. We were discouraged by the inability to do laundry, our boat parts hadn't arrived, the chandlery was closed, and we couldn't buy the needed fresh fruits and vegetables. We were thwarted in everything we tried to do. It was a gray day, and our mood was turning gray as well.

But, when conditions head south, I always think the best thing to do is eat. We ordered a slice of Cod End's famous blueberry pie, a la mode, of course, and a cup of coffee for a little warmth. When the owner served us our pie, it looked so good she returned to the counter to cut a piece for herself. It was a small pleasant moment in an otherwise dreary day, but, things were about to change, change dramatically.

A couple of women came in to buy lobsters. They were discussing shedders versus hard shell. We overheard their conversation and joined in. "Please explain the difference."

"Locals think the shedders are sweeter," they said, "though they don't fill out the shells and have less meat. You can buy a couple of extra ones in order to get enough meat. The shedders also cost less."

"Do you cook them in sea water?" we asked. We're trying to gather information and with it the courage to cook some ourselves on the boat.

"Of course!" they replied. "Without it, they're too bland. And, be sure to add a little seaweed to the water...for flavor. Oh, and don't use too much water. Steam them, don't boil them."

We were intrigued with what we had learned and were ready to try it next time.

"You're cruisers, aren't you?" the women noted.

We looked more like drowned rats than anything else, but "Yes! We're on our sailboat, up here from Florida."

We got to chatting. The one who had introduced herself as Beth had sailed and knew what it was like to be boating in the rain. The discussion included some mention of the closed laundromat and our need to wash, the needed boat parts and then moved on to other topics.

Beth's face lit up with an idea. She said, "Come on home with us. You can wash at our house."

We said a polite "No!" with lots of thanks. It was a generous offer, but we couldn't impose on her kindness.

After a little more conversation, Beth changed her tone. She took charge. What was previously an invitation was now a statement.

"You're coming to the house." That was that! She'd not take no for an answer. "Go back to your boat and get your clothes, we'll wait," she said.

We pointed hesitantly to our soggy boat bags of dirty clothes in the corner, and before we knew it, we were whisked away by mother and daughter for a delightful serendipity.

We crossed the narrow peninsula to Otis Point on the St. George River to "Earthly Heaven," a skillful combination and enlargement of two older, summer cottages at the water's edge. The house overlooked the river, peering between old stately birch trees. It had straight clean lines and a simple elegant beauty. Beth's husband died suddenly about a year ago, and she was readying the house to put it on the market to sell. Her daughter Ann and husband Joe were helping her sort and pack the accumulated "stuff." It was a difficult mix of bitter sweet memories they had to go through.

Earthly Heaven

They bought the place when it was two separate summer cottages. Gradually they rebuilt and upgraded each of the cottages and then joined them together by adding a living room in the middle. The result was a strikingly beautiful, comfortable house with a number of Swedish style built-ins and many skylights. The broad St. George River was visible from every room, through a plethora of windows and doors. Birch trees, their favorites, frame the water's rocky edge. Despite a rather gray day, the windows and skylights made it seem light and airy. Earthly Heaven was decorated with interesting antiques but offered modern comfort. Outside, the traditional cedar shingles gave it its classic Maine charm. It was more than anyone could want for a waterfront home. They named it appropriately, and to their surprise, the township named the road to it, Earthly Heaven Lane, and required them to assign a number to their house. They dutifully posted a "15" on a tree.

Beth got us started washing, built a fire in the fireplace and put us in charge of adding extra wood as needed. After a quick tour of the house, she turned on Glenn Miller for our listening pleasure while she and Ann rejoined Joe to finish cleaning out the garage. We dried out, warmed ourselves in front of the fire and were lulled into a reverie by big band music. Dry and warm, we lazed in luxurious splendor and forgot it was a wet rainy morning.

Just as Bezy finished the last of the wash, Beth returned and invited us to join them for lunch with a salad she had made. The conversation around the table was lively and interesting. Beth's husband was Swedish. They lived in Sweden in their early married life. They cruised on a Motor-sailer, camped on the islands with four small children, and washed clothes in the Baltic Sea. The children were born in Sweden and Switzerland. She knew all about boating in the rain and its difficulties and frustrations. Their daughter Ann had assumed management of the family business, and she and her husband loved sailing. Nowadays they like to charter sailboats in New Zealand when they're not visiting Beth here in Maine.

We were warmed and dried by the fire and warmed by the gift of friendship from total strangers. On the way back to the boat, they stopped by a vegetable stand so we could purchase fresh strawberries, fresh peas, green beans, peaches and tomatoes, at a place we could never have reached by walking.

"Keep in touch with e-mail, and remember, you must stop by on your way back south," Beth called as we headed back toward *Ceilidh* in the dinghy.

What amazing people there are in the world, and how blessed are we to meet so many of them as we cruise. What started as a gray dreary rainy day was turned brighter than sunshine by Beth and Ann who took us in and provided for our needs. It's hard to remember that only a few hours ago we were total strangers. We returned to *Ceilidh* with clean clothes, fresh vegetables and warm hearts.

We put the vegetables and clothes away and settled back in the cabin. The gentle rain tapped lightly on the coach house. The day had a sense of unreality. We pinched ourselves and asked if what had happened really happened, or was it a dream, a mirage? It continued to rain. The fog closed in around us but we scarcely noticed. A warm glow filled the entire boat with a sense of well being.

As darkness fell, the wind backed to the northeast and freshened. The seas that built during the day continued to roll in to the harbor in awkward unsettling swells. The wind and tide held us broadside so we rocked and jerked at the mooring. The rocking motion continued long after the wind died about one o'clock in the morning. I surprised myself by dropping right off to sleep despite the irregular motion. After six years of living on board, I'm finally accustomed to sleeping with lots of uncomfortable movement, as long as my subconscious doesn't detect a change that feels like there might be trouble.

We awoke to a cloudy sky, but before dawn the wind had finally shifted to the southwest and died. The boat once again rode easily at the mooring. I ran the motor to charge the batteries as we had a cup of tea and some breakfast. I overheard men on two trawlers call across to one another, "They don't have *Investor's Daily*, but they have this morning's *Wall Street Journal*." Somehow which financial journal was available seemed the wrong subject for both the moment and the place. I reacted appropriately. I shut the companionway door and put on the water for another cup of tea.

At 10 o'clock, it was time to go to the bicentennial parade for the town of St. George, and the villages of Port Clyde and Tenants Harbor. It was time to celebrate the area that was settled two hundred years ago. Every two-hundred-year-old community has more than enough cause for celebration. Since there were no bleachers or chairs, we took our seats on the curb. The crowd was one deep along the entire parade route. The first music we heard was bagpipes. Right behind the veterans' color guard, leading the parade, was a bagpipe band playing several sets of Scottish music and "America the Beautiful." Then came fire trucks, antique cars, Shriner's midget cars, the Army/Marine National Guard Band, floats by local groups, and buckskin clad frontiersmen with front loading muskets. Kids promoted the local sailing program with a partially rigged sailing dinghy on a truck. Their signs read "I want to learn to sail." The parade ended as St. George towed his dragon on a wagon behind him, subdued and completely under control while everyone waved small flags of St. George. It was great to see people enjoying themselves and having such fun. We watched men tying a half dozen full sections of ribs to a spit for the barbecue. How good that would taste, but the barbecue was for dinner not lunch, and sadly, we needed to move on.

Chapter 9

On to Camden

In the harbor I spotted two Herreshoff twelve-and-a-halfs, a graceful little keel boat, 12.5' on the waterline. Nathanael Herreshoff who designed the famed J boats for the America's Cup, also designed and built 3,000 of these little boats in the early 1900s. The design was so popular that builders replicate it today in fiberglass, but although the hull may be of modern materials, it continues to be fitted with traditional mahogany trim and bronze cleats and blocks. One moored near us was an original Herreshoff boat in exceptional condition, named *Petunia*. Herreshoff designed and built these boats at the request of a group of men who were looking for a safe boat to teach boys to sail. They were originally called Barnegat Bay Boats for Boys. They were designed for the same purpose as the Optimist Prams in which I learned to sail in Clearwater, Florida. One difference between the boats is the first Prams cost $50 in 1947 and the twelve-and-a-halfs cost $400 in 1914. Today a racing Opti costs about $3,200 and the Herreshoff twelve-and-a-halfs sell for nearly $30,000 if they even come up for sale, most often they are bequeathed in a will from a grandfather to a son or grandson.

There was a haze on the water that limited visibility, but we could still see well enough to head for Camden, about 17 miles up Penobscot Bay. As we passed Southern Island, the swells from the open Atlantic were four to five feet on our beam. The misty haze quickly thickened into serious fog. Visibility closed down to four hundred feet. We could make out only the ghostly shapes of the land as we turned north into the Muscle Ridge Channel. The current rushing out the bay towards the Atlantic Ocean ran against us at three quarters of a knot. Visibility continued to drop. Our Garmin 76 global positioning system showed each of the marks and provided us a path. We could make out other boats a hundred or so yards away, just enough to keep out of each other's way. Despite the foggy conditions, there were a number of boats underway. It seems that all the local boats are back in the water for the summer. Everyone is determined to get out regardless of the weather. Because of the fog, we changed our plans and decided to go only as far as Rockland and its large protected harbor.

As we approached Owls Head Cove, however, we noticed the fog was lifting. We could see both shores, and ahead, out in the bay, it was clearing. So again we shifted, reverting to our original destination, Camden. Fog is affected by a number of different conditions, especially air temperature and moisture. The temperature on the bay was enough warmer that the fog was dissipating. In Maine, conditions change quickly. To sail here you need to be flexible, very flexible.

Just ahead, the *Margaret Todd*, a traditional Maine schooner glided gracefully across our bow under full canvas. She is one of the windjammers that takes passengers on week-long cruises through the islands. The traffic lane between Rockland and the Fox Thorofare was crowded with a variety of vessels, island ferries, supply boats taking goods to the islands, and large yachts underway. In addition, there was a gaggle of small and medium sized craft of all descriptions. We picked our way carefully through the congestion and continued up the east side of Penobscot Bay toward Camden.

Off the entrance to Camden Harbor half a dozen 40-footers were jockeying for position at the start of a race. Four Maine schooners, close hauled, tacked in front of us. The sun broke through the clouds, and the last of the fog departed even more quickly than it had come. We picked up a mooring of Wayfarer Marine, the largest marina of this picturesque Maine town that always keeps its welcome mat out for tourists.

Camden Harbor is distinct from others in Penobscot Bay because of what was missing. There were no working lobster boats, only pleasure craft of varying sizes. The tight, inner harbor had moored dock sections to better utilize the limited space. Boats could tie to each side of the anchored dock sections with no need for swinging room. They are called docks, but they are moored out in the bay, not attached to the land and boaters need a launch to get ashore.

The outer harbor was filled with moorings used by sailboats of all types and vintage. Sleek modern racers lay next to classic Sparkman Stephens designs. Among them was another sailboat named *Ceilidh*. We're keeping track and that was only the eleventh "Ceilidh" we've seen in fourteen years. It's always a surprise to find one, almost as unusual as finding someone who can pronounce the gaelic word correctly, *kay-lee*.

The Camden Yacht Club Optimist Pram fleet scooted about between the larger boats as the kids were busy learning to sail. We picked up a mooring and took the launch in to Wayfarer Marine to pay for our mooring and buy some boat parts.

The next day it was time to play tourist! We called the launch on its assigned channel. The driver, a teenager who grew up on the water, drove the launch as a summer job. He pulled skillfully alongside and held his boat tight against ours as we swung a leg over the lifelines and climbed down. The driver steered expertly through the mooring field, picked up other boaters, and dropped us all off at a dock near town rather than at the marina, saving us the mile walk around the end of the harbor.

We wandered among the shops with their crafts, clothes, and trivels ("Trivels" are those trivial things you buy that you don't need, but that catch your fancy and you simply must have them. My niece coined the word on a trip to Europe). A bookstore/coffee shop had jams and jellies made by the Trappist monks at a nearby monastery. We lunched on halibut and finished with ice cream at Boynton-MacKay's...no relation, unfortunately. We found *The Maine Reader*, by editors, Charlie and Samuella Shain, a book we had enjoyed four years ago and were sorry we'd let it get away from us. It's an anthology with poignant stories of Maine life. We wanted to read again a Maine soldier's account of General Robert E. Lee arriving on horseback to surrender his sword, a young woman's description of her grandparent's life in a small Maine cabin, and a piece about E. B. White's house in North

Brooklin, Maine. White was the author of *Charlotte's Web* and other children's stories.

We had left our jars of jam at the store while we walked around, and when we returned to pick them up, there was a sign on the door, "Come out back!" The shopkeeper was on the back patio overlooking the harbor with friends for an afternoon sing-along, accompanied by a flute, guitar and banjo. Other shopkeepers, customers and passersby joined in singing old familiar songs. Bezy and I added some alto and bass to the harmony and had a great time. After about an hour, it was time to go back to work. The musicians dispersed. The shopkeeper got our jams from underneath the counter, and we were off. We'd enjoyed another serendipity that we just stumbled upon.

A ninety-four-foot racing sloop from Great Britain shamed us all by their consummate skill, backing out of the harbor through a veritable mine field of moored boats, and mooring balls. Sailboats are notorious for backing poorly due to their hull configurations and their limited auxiliary power. The British boat had to back out because it was too long to turn around in the crowded harbor. Their backing was an awesome feat of boat handling.

We slipped our mooring and headed out in calm winds and good visibility to motor the eight nautical miles to Rockland.

Chapter 10

Rockland

In contrast to Camden, Rockland is a large, very large by Maine standards, busy, commercial harbor. A number of windjammer passenger schooners were based there. In the old tradition, they hoisted sail in the harbor and sailed out of the confined space, carrying their customers on cruises to a variety of ports around the Bay. They raise sails by hand, singing the traditional sea chanteys to keep in rhythm, just as it was done years ago.

The Maine Ferry Service has ferries that depart from Rockland for the islands, Vinylhaven, North Haven, and Islesboro. The *Island Transporter* leaves from here with building supplies for house construction. We saw it depart with three ready-mix concrete trucks aboard. There's an active fishing fleet of dredgers as well as a fleet of lobster boats that fish from here. Cruising sailors come to provision and take on stores. The Coast Guard Station and a large seafood processing plant dominate the waterfront. The extensive mooring field holds a wide variety of sailboats, while the Atlantic Challenge Foundation teaches the town youngsters to sail in 420s and Optimist Prams as well as teaching wooden boat building. Rockland is especially busy this summer as it has planned to host a Blue's Fest, a Lobster Festival, The Wooden Boat Show, a conventional Boat Show and the Friendship Sloop Regatta.

My favorite memory of the Rockland Harbor was the thirty five Optimist Prams surrounding *Ceilidh* and ghosting past in pea soup fog. The well-trained young skippers handled the demanding situation with skill. A teenager in a skiff watched over them and herded them toward the dock like a border collie. We made our way into the harbor, found a spot to anchor, and dropped the hook.

Knight's Marine has a dinghy dock and is very hospitable to cruisers. We dinghied in to ask if we might use their address to receive a package. The dock master said, "Sure!" Then she noticed *Ceilidh* on Bezy's shirt and turned immediately to point to the wall. There, to our amazement, was our boat card. There was only the single card posted, and it was ours. We had stayed on one of their moorings four years ago. Most cruisers have boat cards, but our card, and only ours was taped up, in lonely splendor, awaiting our return. We were surprised beyond measure. I couldn't recall doing anything that might have made us either famous or infamous. But for some reason we were remembered. They seemed pleased to see us and readily agreed to receive our package.

We came to Rockland to meet Dick and Suzi, the crew of *Charles Ogalin* and to attend the Ocean Cruising Club Rally as their guests. We also wanted to revisit the Farnsworth Museum which houses a number of paintings by N.C. Wyeth, Andrew Wyeth, and Jamie Wyeth. As the museum's collection expanded, they bought an old church and used it to display the additional art they had collected. N.C. Wyeth was primarily an illustrator, well known for his art work in such literary classics as *Treasure Island*, *Robinson Crusoe*, and *The Last of the Mohicans*. Our favorite of the three Wyeths is Andrew, but today, I was taken by a couple of Jamie's paintings of sea gulls. He seems to have captured a character and depth of these ever-present sea birds that show them as more than the raucous, obnoxious beggars they often seem.

Dick and Suzi were here earlier this summer, and helped us find our way around, the way to a laundromat, a short cut to a super market, as well as a place to refill propane tanks. They provided a virtual treasure trove of support services and local knowledge.

Rockland downtown has been revived since our last visit. Bookstores, coffee shops, art galleries, cafes and many other businesses have taken up residence in some of the older buildings. One dress shop had a bank vault as a display area, left over from a previous use of the building. A hair dresser had two exceedingly well trained and gentle wolves, who serve as majordomos at her door. A former optometrist's office was converted to an ice cream parlor. We visited, shopped and ate.

Savoring the distinctive blueberry ice cream, Dick and I agreed that a good project for the summer would be to conduct a "scientific" survey to determine who made the very best blueberry ice cream in all of Maine. To be scientific, it will require extensive sampling of all the ice cream we can find, and to be fair, we must sample them all in sufficient quantity, maybe several times, just to be sure. I sense an ulterior motive to this survey.

Wednesday night we attended the lecture series sponsored by the Island Institute, a not-for-profit group that supports the culture and the well-being of the islands of Maine. The lecture was a hilarious presentation by Phil Crossman from Vinylhaven, reporting on the difficulties the Lion's Club nominating committee had determining who might qualify for King Lion. It's necessary for each candidate to be "from here," only it seems everybody's "from here-ness" has been qualified. A grandfather married a woman who was "from away." And although they immediately moved back "here," their son was then not "from here" because his mother was "from away." She was just "here," despite the fact that she lived "here" all her married life. To be "from here," you have to be born "here." But "here" means born actually on the islands. Matters are further complicated by the fact that no one is actually born on the islands nowadays. Technically, they're all born "away," across the bay in the Rockland Hospital, not actually on the islands themselves. A man's great grandfather was considered to be "from here" despite the fact that he was away for a number of years during the war. Military service doesn't count as being "away." Maybe, they mused, if we developed a point system, with ten points for each relative "from here" and a minus ten points for each relative "from away" that might help. What with the people "from here," the old summer people, the new summer people, and the tourists, it's hard to keep people in the right categories. But if "from here" is not what it used to be, neither is it exactly clear who is "from away" anymore. Finding someone to nominate for King Lion gets more difficult each year. It was hard to tell whether this was a humorous treatment of a serious subject, or a serious treatment of a humorous subject. Phil kept us laughing the entire evening.

Thursday, boats for the Ocean Cruising Club Rally began to arrive. Dick maintains the mailing and e-mail list for the fifteen hundred members of the OCC, a Britain-based group of cruising sailors who qualify for membership by completing an ocean passage of at least a thousand miles on a sailboat under seventy feet in length. Dick qualified when he brought his thirty-two-foot *Charles Ogalin* back across the Atlantic from England where she was built. He offered to sponsor me for membership, based on my qualifying 2,600 mile trip from Kauai, Hawaii to Puget Sound on the thirty-nine-foot sloop, *Red Dog*. His sponsorship is quite an honor.

We went to dinner with Fred and Anne on *Compass Rose*, the Ocean Cruising Club port officers for Annapolis. They regaled us with stories about a trip they made on a cruise ship from Chile, around Cape Horn to Brazil. They rounded The Horn in 50 knot winds in what is considered good weather for that area. The ship had stabilizers, so it didn't roll much from side to side, but did manage to pitch up and down, end to end, with a rather uncomfortable motion. Later, in calm seas off the coast of Brazil, during the first seating for dinner, the ship suddenly turned sharply to starboard and heeled twenty-five degrees. Fred and Anne were in their cabin dressing for the second seating. Anne, in the shower, was bounced back and forth against the shower walls. Fred, an old Navy man, after making sure Anne was okay, headed on deck to see what was happening and whether or not he was needed. As the horizon swung rapidly by and he saw the evening sky instead of the horizon, he realized they were turning hard to starboard at their usual cruising speed of twenty-two knots.

In the dining room, chaos reigned. The multiple place settings of wine glasses went flying, along with the soup course and the silverware. Passengers went into *Titanic* mode and began settling their affairs, heading for the lifeboats, and preparing to meet their maker. Debris in the water was identified as deck chairs, but no one knew whether or not they had been occupied when they slid across the deck and overboard. Slowly the ship righted herself and regained her course. The captain and crew dashed about assessing the damage. A check determined all passengers and crew were still on board. The deck chairs slid overboard without any occupants. There were several broken bones and some contusions but no critical injuries. A computer that ran the ship had fouled up and called for a hard right rudder without bothering to slow the speed first. This was a major computer error, but the results could have been a lot worse. We're familiar with things going wrong on small ships, but on big ships, a small error can have huge consequences. I think we're going to enjoy the new friends of the Ocean Cruising Club. But before the OCC Rally starts tomorrow, there's the always interesting Wooden Boat Show.

At 10 o'clock the next morning, the Wooden Boat Show began, featuring wood working tools and the latest models of boats built of wood as well as antique boats. Wooden canoes, kayaks, and a large variety of other wooden boats were all on display. A completely refurbished wooden Herreshoff twelve-and-a-half was there and offered for sale. The owner noted that Nathanael Herreshoff had sailed an early model that nearly swamped, so he immediately widened the side deck. That bit of information proved that this boat was built quite early, before the change. I managed to resist the bargain price of twenty-six thousand dollars for this jewel. Besides, I don't think she would tow very well behind *Ceilidh* for the nearly eighteen hundred miles back to Florida. Maybe one day...

The wood fabrication and inlay work on the canoes and kayaks was of a top quality. The boats were more works of art than crafts you'd want to commit to the rough and tumble of creeks and streams. One booth demonstrated the "stitch and glue" construction method with a chance for families to build their own small boat during the course of the show. In this construction, you use plastic wire connectors to hold precut, predrilled plywood panels together while you fill the seams with epoxy paste. You then cut away the connectors and fill those holes. With proper bracing and supports you have an easily built, strong, lightweight craft.

Chapter 11

Ocean Cruising Club Rally

At 4 o'clock that afternoon, the Ocean Cruising Club gathered for hors d'oeuvres at the Atlantic Challenge Foundation's boat shed. The members of the OCC represent an impressive accumulation of sailing experience on the seven seas of the world. One member sailed the British Overseas Challenge single handed race around the world. Another was the recent winner of the Marion to Bermuda One-Two Race in which you sail out, single handed, and back with two persons. Everyone present had extensive sailing and blue water experience. It seemed entirely appropriate that the conversation of these mature long distance sailors was accompanied by the hum of sanders and planers at work on the boats under construction by trainees in an adjoining shed. It was an interesting, genial group who welcomed newcomers and greeted old friends warmly. They're the kind of people Bezy and I enjoy being around so I decided to accept Dick's invitation and submit my application for membership. Fred offered to join Dick as a co-sponsor.

The OCC holds rallies in a couple of places in New England and in the Chesapeake each year. Members are scattered up and down the East Coast, through the Caribbean, South America, Australia and around the world. A number of them offer hospitality on their moorings, and there are port officers who welcome OCC cruisers and assist them as they arrive in most important ports world-wide. We'll get to know these cruisers better in the next three days as we've been invited to join them on a mini cruise around Penobscot Bay.

The race for the Thirty & Two Cup was scheduled to begin at 9:00 at the end of the breakwater, an impromptu spur of the moment competition among the three 32' OCC boats. We were all headed toward Smith Cove off Castine on the first leg of the rally. The three boats gathered, mains up, ready to unfurl the jibs,...but there was no wind and the fog got thicker the farther we got from land. Forget racing, it was time to practice our fog skills. We checked on the radio and agreed to continue motoring. On *Ceilidh*, we could barely make out *Charles Ogalin* only two boat length's away, and *Panacea* was visible only as a blip on the radar, just 60 yards farther on.

We were settling in to a routine, steering by a GPS track and watching on the radar for approaching boats, when I spotted a blotch on the radar screen moving towards us at a very fast clip. The first thing we actually saw, a little to starboard, was the sun flashing off a windshield, followed instantly by the shadow of a forty foot powerboat racing past. That boat was too close and too fast. We recovered our composure and stared even harder at the radar. A couple of small, slow moving work boats appeared as no more than ghostly images and moved past, just a little bit off, but there was no more heart-stopping excitement.

Islesboro in ribbon fog.

After a half hour, the fog began to lift. *Charles Ogalin*, emerged from the mist, and we could begin to make out a shadowy *Panacea* in the distance. Gradually the visibility improved. First, the treetops of the islands to our port peeked above the fog. Then, in the distance, we could make out the mountains as they emerged, up behind Camden. They looked like great gray whales rolling in the swells, with their backs rising out of the sea of clouds. Ahead, toward Ilesboro, the departing fog formed ribbons that waved and floated over the trees just before they melted away entirely under the warmth of the morning sun. The bright light of the Maine sunshine illumined *Charles Ogalin's* dinghy with a brilliance and crispness that was a good illustration of the distinct quality of light here, the light that inspires artists and attracts them. Finally, grudgingly, the islands themselves appeared on each side. The day and the setting were typical of why you want to boat in Maine. With the wind on our stern, it warmed. We shed our jackets and enjoyed the sail.

We turned up the river to Castine, and after passing the city docks, turned to the right, into Smith Cove, a large open cove with

Charles Ogalin and *Fatty Knees*

lots of room. The twenty boats of the OCC Rally all anchored at the south end, past the two rock ledges that jut out from either side as the cove narrows. Nearby was Marj's dock. She's the wife of a former member of the OCC. Marj has invited us for steamed mussels as she does each year for the rally. We each brought hor d'oeuvres and a drink for a festive mussel bake on shore. The fresh mussels were still attached to rocks in the cove that morning, then soaked all day in clean water to flush out grit and sand, and finally steamed to perfection in sea water and seaweed as only a long time Mainer can do. We ate and talked...then ate some more...then moved to join a different group to eat and talk. We were still enjoying ourselves when at dark the mosquitoes arrived in droves, chasing us away with hurried "good nights" and back to our boats. A few mosquitoes came aboard on our clothes and nibbled on our legs and arms until we swatted each one personally. The fog of the morning returned to wrap us in a night of quiet muffled sleep.

Morning fog in Smith Cove

The next morning at six, the nearest anchored boat was only a shadowy outline. By seven, the shoreline, Marj's house and dock, and the entire fleet of boats appeared as shadows, just partly visible. By eight, the sun shone brightly on the entire cove.

The morning activity for the rally was a painting class on the dock, taught by Peggy on *Panacea*. All interested artists and would-be artists were invited. Peggy shared lots of insider secrets about painting with watercolors. She believed everyone should paint, just for their own pleasure and enjoyment. Bezy took the painting class while I helped Dick trouble shoot a problem in his pressure water system. On a boat, there's always something to fix or repair. We found the problem, a split in the tank itself, caused by water frozen in it during the severe Massachusetts winter where he stores his boat. He plugged a hose, by-passing the tank temporarily, and got the system working again.

Chapter 12

To Fox Thoroughfare and Perry Creek

Just before noon, the whole Ocean Cruising Club flotilla left Smith Cove in brilliant sunshine for Perry Creek off the Fox Thoroughfare between North Haven and Vinylhaven Islands and another party. As we pulled in our anchor chain, a twist in the chain pushed it off the gypsy, the odd shaped pulley with grooves cut especially to hold the chain, link by link. Uncontrolled, the chain followed gravity over the side and down into the dark green waters of Smith Cove. This had never happened before. But for just such an occasion, in case it ever did, we had spliced a piece of line to the bitter end of the chain and secured that line to a u-bolt in the chain locker. The end of an anchor rode is called the "bitter end" for good reason. It's a bitter experience if the end is not secured to the boat and the anchor and rode goes snaking overboard and is lost. The experience becomes even worse if that is the only anchor and chain you have on board. Today we never reached the bitter end. Other twisted links caught in the windlass gypsy before the entire 160' of chain disappeared over the side. We took a deep breath, recovered our composure, and started again. We didn't lose our anchor, we suffered only a few anxious moments, just long enough to raise our heart rate and for "Murphy" to remind us who was boss.

We followed several of the OCC boats past Castine and turned South into Penobscot Bay. Once again, as we approached the open water of the bay, a wall of fog blanketed the entire reach. A moment ago we were in full sunshine, now visibility is one hundred feet and decreasing by the second, providing us another opportunity to practice "transit in fog" skills.

Our GPS had a trackback feature that guided us back along the path we came yesterday. We steered along that line. The track back, however, covered only the first half of the passage. The radar, set on a range of three quarters of a mile, showed who was moving nearby, and we blew our trusty conch as a fog horn, one long blast at one-minute intervals to warn others of our presence.

I engaged the autohelm, known affectionately as Angus MacHelm, our hardest working crew member with a minimum of complaining or grouching. Angus was also cheap to feed, just stuff in a few amps every hour. For the 12-mile stretch across open water, Angus took us from waypoint to waypoint without difficulty. That left the rest of the crew, Bezy and me, to focus on not hitting anything and keeping a close watch so that nothing that appeared suddenly out of the fog hit us. Blips appeared on the radar screen and moved across it. If they headed along the edge without approaching "us" in the center, we didn't worry. If they crossed the screen from side to side, we watched closely to make sure we didn't meet in the middle. It was those that appeared at the top and headed directly toward the center, where we were, that got our closest attention. We never saw boats that we noted on the radar only thirty yards away. We knew they were there, only as a moving radar blip and the muffled thrum of their motor.

Suddenly, a sailboat burst into view about thirty yards off our bow with a spinnaker flying and closing fast. We never saw it on the radar. The captain was snuggled comfortably back in the cockpit, smoking a cigar. He smiled and waved as he passed, close enough to reach over and shake hands. "Fog? What fog? Who's worried? Not me!"

A few boats overtook us from behind, but they approached more slowly since we were all going the same direction. Our procedure was to note the blip on the radar, determine which way it was moving and how fast, judge whether or not its track would bring it close, prepare to take evasive action and alert them with a horn signal. It was a busy, stressful time. But, with Angus at the helm, a GPS to guide us, and radar to avoid "things that go bump in the fog" we finally got into a groove and managed to miss everything that came at us. The fog teased us twice about lifting, but it quickly returned each time, thick as ever.

We picked up Drunkard Ledge on the GPS at the entrance to Fox Thoroughfare, rounded the red can, and turned up the reach, hoping that when we approached the land, the fog would lift. It didn't. The Fiddler's Ledge stone monument marking the ledge to the west showed on both the GPS as a mark and on the radar as an image, but we never laid eyes on it. We were less than thirty yards off and didn't see a thing, not even a shadow. Lobster boats appeared out of the dark fog curtain, racing towards us at 14 knots and passed close by. A ferry blasted its fog horn as its ghostly shape loomed above us on our starboard bow. As I started to steer away from the ferry, Bezy motioned to the shadowy outline of a mega yacht very close on our port. We were in the middle of the channel with boats all around us and the visibility was measured in feet.

We were already jumpy when, suddenly, the depth sounder dropped to 6', then 5' and the shallow water alarm blared. "Rocks!" we thought...Maine "granite sharks" that take a bite out of keels. Throttle back...out of gear...brace for the crunch of the keel hitting the rock...double check the chart...confirm we're in the middle of the channel...confirm there were no rock ledges in the middle of the channel...at least none showing on the chart. We haven't hit anything...yet. The alarm stopped. The depth changed to 8', then 10', then 18' and 35'. Take two deep breaths, and signal the heart to resume beating. Shift into forward gear...add a little throttle...check the depth sounder again. It's reading 40.' Resume breathing.

Sometimes, when the bottom is soft, or when power boats churn up the water and aerate it, the depth sounder loses its signal and gives false readings. This is definitely not the time for such nonsense. It seems that's what just happened, a trick played on the captain by the instruments.

Finally, looking forward, the fog was lifting as the land closed from each side. In no time we moved out of it entirely, and the sun shone on the boats moored on both sides. Lobster boats were on the move, all coming toward us at full throttle. From comments we overheard on the VHF Radio we learned that there was a lobster boat race today in Deer Thoroughfare. It was now over and everyone was heading home. In place of the usual piles of lobster traps on the stern, there were grills and folding chairs. Family and friends replaced the crew and working gear. It was a festive time, a day of rest from the arduous work of pulling the traps, removing the "bugs," re-baiting the traps and re-setting them to catch more lobster.

We turned to the south, around Hopkins Point and into Perry Cove. This was a small Maine cove with all the features you'd expect, crystal clear water, rocky shores marked by kelp below the tide line, and an irregular shoreline with spruce trees stretching skyward. When we tried to anchor, the anchor chain was badly twisted, so wadded up that the wads were too big to pull out through the hawser pipe. There was little room to circle in the snug creek while I went below, stretched the chain out on the v-berth and spent the 20 to 30 minutes required to straighten it out. If we could get settled first, then we could untwist the chain at our leisure.

There was an unoccupied mooring nearby so we poached it, ready to leave if the owners came around, or if nobody showed, we would use it for the night. It had been a busy day. We'd burned a lot of nervous energy and were tired, so we decided to forego the party ashore. I stretched out on the couch and slept soundly until it was time to wake up and officially go to bed at ten o'clock. Again the fog drew a thick curtain around the boat and snuggled us in for the night. We said a heartfelt "thank you" to the mooring's owner whoever he was, thankful that we could wait until morning to straighten out our anchor chain, and thankful that we could sleep securely and recover from an exciting day in the Maine fog.

After going to bed with fog so thick you could wad up a ball of it and throw it to shore, we awoke to a bright, if cloud strewn morning. Streaks of pink and mauve brushed across the clouds and reflected on the water. The rocky shoreline of Perry Creek was topped by pointed conifers all around. We had tea in the cockpit as we began to think about considering whether or not to consider beginning to think about starting the day.

Chapter 13

Back to Rockland and the Friendship Sloop Races

After breakfast, it was time to deal with the anchor chain and unwind its twists and turns, putting it back in order. I pulled the entire 160' of chain out and laid it on a towel on the V-berth, untwisting it as I went. The last 14' were a tight mass of links curled back on one another. At this point I untied the 10' length of nylon rode from the u-bolt in the chain locker so it could finally unwind. I have never figured out how chain gets twisted so badly, nor has anyone been able to explain it to me. For it to twist this much, the boat would have to circle and circle and circle around the anchor which just doesn't happen. How does it get twisted? Someday I may figure it out.

With the chain straightened and returned to the anchor locker, we were ready to get underway. Rockland is about 12 miles to the west, across West Penobscot Bay. We headed back out the Fox Thoroughfare where we had come yesterday in the fog. We had seen none of the thoroughfare coming in from the bay yesterday. All we saw was gray, gray shadows, gray curtains, gray mist. This morning, navigating was simple. We could see. Our trackback line on the GPS indicated we'd come within 100' of the stone column marker on Fiddler's Ledge which we could now see clearly in the daylight. The depth sounder acted up again, at the exact same place as yesterday. It seems the bottom there was soft and didn't "echo back" the depth sounder's signal. We were never in danger of running aground or hitting a rock, but we had no way of knowing that then.

Everyone was enjoying the great weather for sailing, windjammers, cruising yachts, small sailboats and a Friendship Sloop, tuning up for the races, a couple of days away. We had a beam reach across to Rockland in 15 knot winds. The Rockland harbor, off in the distance, was covered in mist, but there was no fog. We slipped past the lighthouse at the end of the long breakwater, found a suitable spot and dropped anchor. Our patient straightening of the anchor chain allowed it to run out smoothly. An all chain anchor rode was important in Maine where the tides were 10' and you were anchoring in deep water. Chain also allows for good holding in a smaller swinging circle. That allows you to anchor safely in more crowded places. And in addition, as the boat swings back and forth dragging the chain across the rocks on the bottom, a chain rode won't chafe itself in two.

Dick and Suzi arrived in Rockland an hour later and anchored nearby. They had spent the previous night in Buck's Harbor and sailed in from there. That evening we joined the gathering of the Friendship Sloop Society on the town dock, and ten of us went to dinner together. When she had finished a beef pot pie with Stilton cheese, Bezy couldn't resist her favorite desert, apple crisp. The serving was so large that I had to take my spoon and help out. It took both of us to "do it justice."

Friendship Sloops derived their name from Friendship, Maine where the boats were built from 1880 to 1920. They were designed to handle the inshore fishing and lobstering. They have gaff rigged mains with a jib and staysail and sometimes a topsail to add canvas aloft when the winds are light. Their cockpits were large and open, in order to "hold the catch." To work a lobster trap, a sloop would approach the buoy close hauled, slack the sails as they hooked the buoy, using the boat's momentum to run up the buoy line to the trap. With the sails slack, the boat lay quietly in place while the lobsterman hauled the trap, removed the lobsters, rebaited the trap, and put it back in the water, an operation taking about three minutes. Some of the sloops' design enhanced this maneuver and made them especially suited for work in close quarters. Despite being broad of beam with a full keel, they are nimble as well as sturdy, ideal qualities for working traps inshore with shoal water and smaller spaces. They were replaced as work boats when gas and diesel engines replaced sail.

A few of these classic boats survive but many have been lost. The society maintains a list of all known hulls and encourages and assists anyone interested to find an original hull and restore it. In the 1970s they began building fiberglass hulls, making the fiberglass mold using a classic boat as the plug. The molded hulls were then fitted out with wooden decks, spars and cabinetry and rigged with traditional solid spars and heavy canvas sails.

The Friendship Sloop Society is a hearty, dedicated group of sailor/craftsmen who rebuild and maintain these sturdy graceful working sailboats from Maine's history. The Society boasts strong family traditions, and frequently the whole family takes part in the race. It was fascinating to walk the docks and see a racing crew that included very young children, teenagers, young adults and older retirees. Boats are often passed down within the family from one generation to the next. Many members of the Society have been friends and sailed together for years. Yet the Friendship Sloops constantly attract newcomers, young couples up for an adventure and persons just retired ready for a project they've dreamed about for years. The weather-worn faces and strong roughened hands speak of the hard work required to sail and own these historic wooden craft. It was a distinct honor for us to sail and race with these very special men and women.

Some of the sloops rafted together at the dock had museum quality varnished woodwork. A few, however, looked like the original rough and weathered work boats they once were. Many boats had been restored and maintained by their owners with thousands of hours spent in the shed behind their homes. Lawyers, accountants, engineers, tradesmen, and bankers learned a myriad of boat building skills in order to make their dreams come true. Some of the hulls are 100 years old and are still seaworthy and strong.

Banshee II, and *Gaivota*, our friends' boats, had a furniture-like finish on their solid spruce spars and gleaming varnish on all their bright work. We've been invited to sail with Bill and Kathy Whitley on *Gaivota*. Gaivota is Portuguese for a small tern, the mythical bird that leads one to heaven.

The weather predictions for the regatta were not good. Storms, wind, fog and rain were all expected. But this was Maine and these sloops were Maine working boats, so what was the problem? We were up early, packed our lunch and foul weather gear, and gathered for the skipper's meeting to receive instructions for today's race. Before race announcements, however, the Society recognized its officers and committee chairs, new members, and local people who help make the race week possible. In addition to the traditional officers and committees...president, vice-president, secretary, etc., the Society's non-traditional officers were recognized... Inspector of Mast Wedges, a Cannoneer, and a Piper. I said it was a unique group.

The Race Committee described the possible courses it might use, clarified the starting sequence, and settled on VHF Channel 72 for communication. Instructions in hand, everyone departed to the boats.

Friendship Sloop Regatta 2013
Photo courtesy Friendship Sloop Society

The mood today was more somber than usual. Two years ago in uncertain weather, one boat was dismasted. Another took a lot of water in the cockpit that sloshed forward inside the hull. With all that weight forward, the boat dove beneath the waves and sank. All crew members were safely rescued and the boat was later raised, but memory of that day has injected a note of caution and extra concern when there is bad weather. The Friendship Sloops are stout seaworthy boats designed for Maine weather, but they are not invincible. A line of squalls accompanying a warm front was approaching from the south and headed our way. The Race Committee delayed the start of the race until the front had passed. Unperturbed by the delay, everyone used the time to visit with friends, or to move about the dock and check out the other boats.

After 45 minutes, radar indicated the squall line had broken up and was no longer a threat. So the end boat cast off its lines and one by one the other boats took their lines on board and headed out to the race course on the outer edge of the harbor.

The southwest wind was 12 to 15 knots, gusting to 20. The fog limited visibility to one-eighth of a mile, and the race was held inside the breakwater because of the blustery uncertain weather. With a predicted 20 knots of wind, we tied in a single reef before we left the dock. *Gaivota*'s diesel throbbed to life. I took the wheel while Bill raised the huge gaff-rigged mainsail displaying both his experience and his muscle. The boat is 31' long on the deck, but with the bow sprit extending forward and the main boom hanging out over the stern, it measures 50' overall. You have to marvel at a Maine fisherman handling a boat like this by himself in addition to fishing. Sometimes, though, he'd tow a skiff which he fished from while a young boy "jogged" the sloop back and forth nearby.

Launching a new boat
Photo courtesy Friendship Sloop Society

We checked in with the Committee Boat and jockeyed amidst the other racers, waiting for the starting sequence to begin. The ten minute gun sounded, and we set our watches. Exactly ten minutes later the starting gun fired, and we were off. We got a good start and were moving nicely, close to the buoy end of the line, just behind a couple of other boats. Bill was at the helm. Bezy and Suzi tended the jib. Dick handled the GPS, radio and other electronics, and I tended the mainsheet. We were not overly serious about racing because of our handicap. It's hard to sail fast when the boat's so heavy. *Gaivota* is set up for comfortable cruising which means extra weight in bedding and other creature comforts. In addition, Bill carries enough spare parts to build a second sloop.

Gaivota, a Friendship Sloop
Photo courtesy Friendship Sloop Society

He is generous helping other boats in need and carries tools and parts for many situations. On the gusts we heeled and shipped a bit of water on the side deck. We furled and unfurled the jib to delete and add sail as the wind increased and slackened. Finally, the fog lifted so we could see the entire harbor. The front stalled out and didn't affect us at all. There was an occasional drop or two of rain, but never more than a few at a time. It was a fine sail with genial people in a classic sailboat.

Back at the dock, as we relaxed with a glass of wine, Bill regaled us with tales of commercial fishing in his off hours as a naval officer stationed in Alaska. In the Gulf of Alaska they faced mountainous seas and gale force winds most of the time, but the fish and crab were plentiful and the pay was good.

At four, there was a rowing race with the dinghies. The rower was blindfolded and his navigator was not allowed to speak, he could only touch a knee or shoulder to give directions and to guide the oarsman down the course. The results were hilarious. Dinghies scattered all over the east end of the harbor. The real surprise of the race was that any of the racers were able to finally make it across the finish line after much knee tapping and shoulder pushing.

Wednesday dawned with fog, washed down with a drizzling rain. The race was postponed. It was a good day to be boat bound, a good day to start slowly with a cup of coffee in a warm dry cabin. We talked with Bill on the radio. He's not planning to race, even if the race is rescheduled. He's helping Dick with a project on Dick's boat. But first, Bill canvassed the town in search of a hard-to-find bronze part needed for the job.

Mid-day, the weather improved, and the Friendship Sloops decided to race. They did a "Start from Anchor" in which each boat anchors near the starting line and waits for the starting gun. When it sounds, you have to put up the sails, pull the anchor, and get underway. It's not easy to begin sailing from anchor, nor is raising the large heavy sails something you can do in a hurry. "Start from Anchor" involves skills that are not often required of racers, but the skills were required to fish from these sloops. Once again I was reminded these are not usual boats or your usual sailors.

That night we attended another of the Island Institute Lecture Series, a presentation on Movies Made in Maine. Hollywood comes on location in Maine to get authentic reality, but then proceeds to doctor that reality to suit their images of what "real Maine" looks like, or should look like...according to Hollywood. The people "from here" chuckle all the way to the bank with the money Hollywood provides the economy, millions of dollars for a couple of minutes of film that makes it to the screen. The director built a scale model of a Maine dock in an Arizona water park for *The Perfect Storm*, and he rebuilt two blocks of the main street of Southwest Harbor, in a warehouse in Canada. Why not just shoot the scenes here? Practical Mainers are left in total disbelief as they marvel at the silliness, but the money's good.

Afterwards, we went to a sing-along sponsored by the Friendship Sloop Society, relaxed, laid back fun. After the singing, one of the boaters who had written a children's book about his dog sailing on the boat, read it to the 35 children gathered.

Thursday dawned with more fog. We should be getting accustomed to it by now. We gathered for breakfast at the Rockland Cafe, to fortify ourselves for a strenuous day on the water. The rain hovered nearby. Today's start was traditional. The boats maneuver in back of a 200-yard line between a buoy and the Committee Boat. The line was set perpendicular to the wind direction. There was a ten minute starting sequence, counting down to the start. The ideal start is to sail full speed toward the line and to reach it a fraction of a second after the starting gun fires. Friendship Sloops are heavy boats with lots of sail. It takes them awhile to reach full speed, but they are equally hard to slow down once they get going. We were driving for the line, in great position, only we were a little early, and we couldn't slow. We crossed the line three seconds before the starting gun sounded. When that happens you have to turn around, go back, and restart, staying out of everybody else's way as you struggle to make it back through the congestion. Bill recovered nicely and after restarting, had *Gaivota* sailing well. We covered a couple of boats on starboard tack, blocked their wind and passed them.

The second lap around the course, we tacked inshore and got a favorable wind while some boats on the edge of the harbor hit a flat spot. Bummer for them. We cheered for John and Carol as they led the usual winner. It was another great day on the water, good sailing and pleasant people.

We celebrated with dinner at the Black Pearl. As we waited to be seated, Andre, the resident seal, swam up to the dock looking for a handout. He stared up at us with his big black eyes. Although they are an attraction to tourists, locals know seals as rascals that cause more trouble than they're worth, breaking into traps, fouling lines, and in general, making a nuisance of themselves. Someone had sighted a beluga whale in the harbor earlier, so we scanned several times to see if we could get a glimpse of him. Evidently he had gone elsewhere.

We had a great experience sailing on historic craft with expert sailors and craftsmen. We enjoyed the fellowship of The Friendship Sloop Society and their warm welcome. This group seems typical of both Maine's passions and its hospitality.

Friday, most of the Friendship Sloops departed for home, and it was time for us to tend to our needs. On a boat, you must provide for everything yourselves. There are no water mains, electrical lines, or other power source to connect to. It was time to wash the five bags of dirty laundry, take on groceries, fill the propane tanks, top off the diesel, and check our water supply. It was a bit more difficult than it sounds because we were at anchor and all this had to be done by dinghy, carrying everything back and forth to the boat. In addition, we had no land transportation so we walked wherever we went. We did have a folding cart which helped considerably.

First, we carried our laundry up the steep hill to the laundromat. Bezy began the washing while I returned to the dinghy for the propane tanks. Finding a place to refill propane is not always easy, but today we were lucky. There was a filling station right across from the laundromat that sells propane, and a Hannaford's Grocery a block up the street where we could buy groceries.

After returning the three full tanks to the dinghy, I headed for the grocery store, armed with a list. Today the list was bigger than my ability to carry, even with the hand cart. I piled the cart high with three boat bags overflowing with cans and boxes and struggled to carry seven plastic bags of fruits and veggies, rolls and bread in my two hands, with the toilet paper pack tucked under my arm. I just made it the block to the laundromat before my grip gave out, and I dropped the bags on the sidewalk. Bezy and I were gathering all the bags together to carry them the three remaining blocks to the dinghy when a lady, waiting for her laundry to finish said, "Do you need a ride?" My first response was "No thank you!"

but I instantly realized that was a lie, and before the words were out of my mouth, I called them back and changed my answer to a relieved, "That would be terrific." We loaded our groceries in the back seat and she whisked us away to the dock. Helping angels appear at the most opportune time.

Fully loaded, the dinghy rode quite low in the water, unusual for an Inflatable with its big inflated tubes, but I got the groceries and propane on board *Ceilidh* and went back for Bezy and the laundry. It was only 2:30 and we had "killed a bear," an old Georgia saying for getting a lot accomplished.

Condensation made the boat sopping wet on the inside. The moisture in the air and the warming temperatures had left condensation on every inside surface. It felt like the boat was filled with damp fog. The fog had moved inside and settled in every cabinet and locker. The sun was out. The breeze was up. So we opened the ports and hatches to let the air funnel through with hopes of drying things out.

I went in to mail a package and to send e-mail, my laptop under my arm. The local library had a place to plug in a phone line so you could send and receive e-mail. Libraries are a wonderful resource with a variety of helpful services which are often under used by both boaters and by people on the land. Exiting the library, my gait changed when I saw the dark clouds filling in rapidly from the northwest. If I hurried, I might make it back to the boat before the storm broke. I jumped in the dinghy, powered up the outboard and managed to secure the dinghy's painter to the cleat on *Ceilidh*'s transom, just as the wind freshened on the front edge of the rapidly approaching storm. It was the first significant thunderstorm we'd encountered in Maine, with winds of 30 knots and bolts of lightning crashing nearby. Thank goodness, most of the lightning hit on the land to our north.

Ceilidh sails on her anchor, switching from side to side. Sometimes when she gets broadside to the wind it puts enough strain on the anchor to break it out. At times like these, she has dragged. We would most likely be fine in these conditions, but I preferred a bit of prevention, especially since we have friends anchored astern as well as all the mooring balls, lobster traps and a variety of other hazards that are lying downwind. I powered up and maintained enough headway to hold the boat in place, putting it in and out of gear, accelerating and steering to keep the bow into the wind and the strain off the anchor rode. The crab trap that was dropped right beside us after we anchored, the one that had banged repeatedly against the side of the boat during the night, now served a useful purpose. It gave a point of reference as I maneuvered in place. I used it to confirm I was holding and not dragging.

As expected, the storm passed in about 15 minutes. I was wet through and through by the cold rain, but we were still in the place where we started. I powered down, and *Ceilidh* lay back gently on her anchor. A rainbow went from horizon to horizon off our stern, the biblical promise to never again destroy the earth by flood.

As the sunshine returned, Dick and Suzi came over for refreshments. We'll go separate ways in the morning. Their warmth, generosity and love of fun have contributed a lot to the enjoyment of our trip thus far. We are blessed to have them as friends.

Chapter 14

To Southwest Harbor, via the Fox and Deer Island Thoroughfares

We headed across Penobscot Bay toward the Fox Island Thoroughfare between Vinalhaven and North Haven Islands. The frontal passage during the night had cooled the air. The sun was out. The sky was clear. Without any haze we could see the whole panorama of islands, as far off as distant Mount Desert. The water sparkled as if crystals were scattered across it. It's easy to understand why Penobscot Bay has a reputation as one of the loveliest parts of the Maine coast. We could tell it was time to head east because the wind was coming from the east, the exact direction we wanted to go. "Wind on the nose," the inevitable fate of sailors.

A coastal schooner made sail and left the harbor with us, ghosting along, close-hauled. Everyone was out enjoying the improved weather. Today's sunshine was in stark contrast to the rain and fog that plagued us all last week. It was a beam reach across lower Penobscot Bay, the best and easiest point of sail, and everyone had their sails set.

The Fox Island Thoroughfare is a narrow pass between several islands with a constant flow of traffic and lots of boats moored along each side. Small craft of all sorts bobbed and bounced from the wakes of the boats "just passing through." The moored boats often obscured the navigation marks which made for an exciting time for boats under sail in this confined area. The communities ashore represented Maine at its best. The houses were sided with cedar shingles. The shorelines were lined with rocks large and small. Conifers pointed upwards in every open space. Large homes overlooked the harbor from both sides. The ferry dock, with its steel structure to lift the ramp and adjust it for tidal changes, dominated the north side.

As we cleared the congested area, the passage was dotted by smaller, uninhabited islands whose rocky points continued out underwater as ledges. The water was quite deep in most places, except for those rocks scattered here and there. It's essential for boaters to know exactly where "here and there" are.

At the end of the Fox Thoroughfare, there was a four-mile stretch of open water before you passed between Deer Island and Isle Au Haut. For those four miles you crossed the open water of East Penobscot Bay. The Atlantic Ocean was to the south, and we felt the ocean swells caused by the winds of the past few days in far off places. The boat rose and fell in an easy motion as the swells passed under. Lobstermen worked their traps off the islands. The sun lit the exposed rocks and shone through the trees with a rich variegated palette of greens. One could hardly resist taking up a brush in a feeble attempt to replicate the myriad shades of green and the patterned beauty of the trees. Post card photographers get extremely frustrated deciding which of the hundreds of views to share with the public and which ones might sell best.

As we entered Deer Thoroughfare, on the right we saw the rusted crane from the Stonington granite works where much of the granite used in buildings in Boston, New York City and Washington, DC was quarried. The granite was shipped out on sailing schooners around the turn of the century. A number of squared off blocks line the shore, waiting patiently for transport which will likely never come, and any boats that do come, will certainly not be powered by sail. That era has passed. A nearby island was piled with smaller granite blocks abandoned there, stained brown by the salt water and by the algae growing on them.

Like Fox, the Deer Thoroughfare was lined with moored boats, sailboats of all size and vintage, as well as the lobster boats which are moored close to the traps they work and close to the homes of the lobstermen.

A windjammer with its passengers disappeared behind an island to the north, into an area where the chart shows rocks and ledges and only a narrow unmarked channel. They obviously had the required local knowledge, for in a few minutes they emerged

Windjammer leaving Rockland

serenely on the other side on their way to Blue Hill Bay. The wind built to 20 knots as we sailed into Jericho Bay, past Egg Rock, and picked up the marks for the Casco Passage. I can't tell you how comforting it was to actually see marks rather than only feel for them in the fog. Even with the aid of the GPS and radar, seeing with the eyes was so much better and much, much easier on the psyche. There were many small islands that made up the southern edge of this thoroughfare. Not only did they provide a different look, but they also offered different experiences for a variety of boaters. A moaning horn on an island welcomed us, a very useful navigation aid, one that was reassuring in good light, as a reminder that it was there if needed.

A bevy of kayakers crossed our bow. The protected waters between the islands is great for kayakers, and the small Maine islands are interesting places to explore. All kinds of boats fit in Maine's varied waters. This area provides each kind with its own special set of challenges and delights.

As always the lobster pots dotted the water like three dimensional confetti floating on it. It took constant attention to avoid them, and on occasion they distracted one from one's navigation. A navigational error here was not the "Oops!" of grounding on sand in Florida. It was a real "crunch and shudder" that could do serious damage to the keel and rudder. Again, we were impressed by the charts and how helpful they were navigating in a new area. Their detail and accuracy was impressive. I wished there were midscale charts that showed the larger picture and allowed one to better transition from a smaller more detailed chart to the next adjacent one. Until you got a feel of the area, it was difficult planning and following a route, difficult to make the transition from one page to the next.

We anchored in a cove John had marked for us, between Case, Devil's and Bald Islands. The entrance was clear since the rocks at the entry were above water at near low tide. We put out 100' of chain for the 25' depth and settled back to enjoy the view. Small boats sailed into the cove, then sailed out again. Two large canoes with twelve young campers headed for their home camp on Devil's Island. We had spotted their tents back in the trees as we arrived. Later in the evening a dozen kayaks passed with older campers headed in the same direction. We couldn't tell whether they were parents just arriving, or some enterprising camp program that attempted to combine seniors with kids. I chose to believe the latter.

The crew of another boat that had anchored nearby dinghied over to visit. To our surprise, they announced that their boat was also named *Ceilidh*. I think it was the boat we saw on the mooring in Camden. George, the owner, was a charming Mainer who had cruised these waters for 30 years. He too works with the Maine Island Trails Association, the same group our friend John Towne helps. The Association publishes a book of trails that are available for public use. It also supervises their use for camping and day use by small boats.

In the last four days we have met four people who know how to pronounce Ceilidh. We've kept count for the last ten years, and that brings the total to twenty. Maybe we should have selected a better known name, one easier to pronounce. Nah! It's a good name, and we like what it represents, the best of Scottish hospitality, the gathering in the pub on a Friday evening with music and dancing, and a "wee bit o' Scotch."

We spent a peaceful night listening to music and reading. The half-moon lit the water with a path you felt you could walk on. Just step off the boat and walk across the water...straight up to the sky...all the way up to the moon itself. The path was still there in the middle of the night when I roused to go to the head. The moon and the moonlight are always welcome companions in the middle of the night on a boat at anchor.

We made little forward movement the next day. We travelled only far enough to drop our anchor in the cove off Buckle Island, in deep water close to the north end of the island. But since the most direct channel was unmarked, we elected to approach from the green mark in the Casco Passage. It was a little farther, but it was safer. A half-dozen boats had found this cozy anchorage before we did, but they left a spot for us with enough room to swing between four other boats. On our port was a 24' sloop named *Flicka*. *Flicka's* crew was a couple and their dog who peeked over the cockpit combing, watching everything happening in the harbor. The other boats' crews had gone ashore in their dinghies to explore the shoreline, waiting for the tide to recede far enough for them to gather mussels. In the meantime, they enjoyed land time off the boat. Their dogs especially enjoyed a frisky romp along the beach, chasing each bird that dared to light on the sand.

A sixty foot, very, very new trawler from New Brunswick dropped anchor in our midst, way too close to all the boats. When you hear the rattle of chain clattering over the side, you get a feel of how close a boat is without needing to come up on deck to see.

The lady on *Flicka* commented, "I feel like David, of David and Goliath."

"Have you got your slingshot?" I asked.

The trawler dragged down on the anchor float of one of the boats and was about to tangle the float line in its prop. I called in a loud voice and informed the trawler's captain of the danger. To the relief of all, he pulled his anchor and moved off to another location. It took three more attempts for him to get his anchor set properly with enough rode out and with swinging room that wouldn't endanger other boats. It was pretty clear this was a new boat with a new Captain. All it takes to buy a big boat is a check book. You can't buy the training needed to handle it. That has to be earned by experience, and experience costs time.

The fading sun painted the trees and the sky with its multicolored brush, tints of orange, pink and mauve. The mountains of Mount Desert arched in the background. When darkness settled in, it was quite dark. The only lights we could see were the anchor lights of nearby boats, tiny dots that tend to blend with the starlit night sky. It's hard to believe the profound dark we're experiencing in Maine. Nowadays we live with so many electric lights, it's hard to find a spot that doesn't have at least some ambient light. The price we pay for our twenty-four hours of light is we miss the magic of the starry night sky in its sparkling brilliance, and the isolation and profundity of true darkness.

The weatherman called for showers accompanied by high winds for the day. When we awoke, the rain had not yet arrived nor had the winds, but there was a haze and a hint of fog. We pulled the anchor and moved north and east toward Southwest Harbor on the southern shore of Mount Desert Island. We completed the Casco Passage and turned east toward Bass Harbor Bar, toward the narrow break in the ledge where it's deep enough for us to cross. A flashing red sector of the lighthouse on Bass Harbor Head sent us scrambling for our charts. A red sector indicates there is danger on your current heading. Your approach is leading you towards a shoal. The lighthouse guides boats north out of the bay east of Swan's Island, so the white sector is a narrow one coming up from the southeast. We turned a little to starboard and found the narrow channel and its marking buoys and proceeded safely through.

The rounded domes of the mountains of Mount Desert were blue gray in the morning haze. It was hard to guess the weather's ultimate plans for the day, but it appeared any bad weather would hold off long enough for us to make it to Southwest Harbor, just eight miles away. Visibility closed down to a little less than a mile, but after our previous fog experience, seeing only shadows at 30 yards, a mile's visibility seemed almost generous. Nevertheless, we were relieved to enter the security of the large, busy Southwest Harbor.

Southwest Harbor

Chapter 15

Southwest Harbor

Three-fourths of the moorings in Southwest Harbor were filled with Hinkleys, not surprising since the home office of Hinkley Boats is here. The concentration will be even higher in two weeks when the 75th Anniversary Hinkley Rally is held. We sailed through the mooring field admiring first this boat then another, especially the sleek, classic, Hinkley Bermuda Forty, an elegant yacht. We spotted *Joye*, Bob and Shirley Zinn's boat. The Zinns are friends from Clearwater, Florida. *Joye* was just recently launched for the season and has not yet moved from the Hinkley mooring to the Zinns' private one at the head of the harbor. We tried to hail Beal's Lobster House to rent one of its three moorings, but they weren't monitoring the VHF, nor could we raise the harbormaster to inquire about the city moorings.

While we figured out where we would stay, we tied up at the Hinckley dock to take on fuel and water. The dockmaster persuaded us to take one of their moorings and assigned us one, down the harbor from the company floats and shore installation, directly in front of Bob Hinckley's house.

The Zinns came by and invited us up to see their new condo on the west end of the harbor. By the time we got ashore, the sun came out and the wind freshened. Any thought of rain or fog seemed far away as we scanned the whole harbor from the vantage point of their porch. From there, we overlooked the entire mooring field, the entrance to Somes Sound, and Northeast Harbor in the distance. The view from the back of the condo was equally intriguing. It was a forested area where Bob had created a snowshoe path up into the woods for winter use. Harbor in the front, forest in the back...an amazing place to live.

Next morning, the fog returned, so there was no rush to venture out. We enjoyed a second cup of coffee but the fog was still thick as ever. Grudgingly, we admitted the fog had won, and we would wait no longer, we'd go ahead with our morning plans in the fog. We set out in zero visibility to check out the brand new West Marine store at the head of the harbor. I took my handheld GPS and marked the mooring as a waypoint so we could find our way back.

After checking out West Marine, we peeked in the other shops, enjoyed stretching our legs, got the bus schedule for the Acadia National Park Transporter, and had an ice cream cone before reversing our tracks back to the dock. By the time we reached our dinghy, the sun had broken through the clouds and was drying up the fog. We could see *Ceilidh* from the north shore, lying comfortably on her mooring on the opposite side of the harbor.

Next day, we went ashore and took the park bus to Bar Harbor. A cruising couple we met on the street told us about this bus service the Acadia National Park operates throughout the park. The bus not only provides transportation but, in the process, provides a tour of the entire Island, past Eagle Lake, Somes Sound, and all the park's campgrounds. We got on board and were off to the "big city."

In Bar Harbor we shopped and ate. We bought a pillow filled with balsam boughs to bring the aroma of the Maine forests inside the boat. Bezy spotted a sweatshirt with a polo player monogram on it, astride a Moose. We laughed for three blocks at the spoof of the Ralph Lauren logo. We walked along the path by the water in front of the stately old homes, and watched a four-masted schooner *The Margaret Todd* make sail. After a fun-filled day, we boarded the bus for home.

Nancy and Ron of *Always Saturday* got Hinckley to varnish their teak. They were doing some of the simpler tasks themselves, working alongside of the varnishers, and learning a lot about Hinckley's approach. They promised to share what they learned. Hinckley does an outstanding job with maintenance, and use it as a part of their most effective business model. Part of what they sell with their boats is a standard of maintaining them. They welcome their "chicks" back to the Hinckley nest each winter for major repair and rehab in their heated storage and work shed. This model provides quality maintenance on their boats, protects the owner's summer sailing time on the water, and keeps Hinkley's income up during the winter months, giving year-round employment to their workers. We picked up a copy of the book Hinckley published about boat maintenance. The book's slogan is, "Not every boat can be a Hinckley, but they can each be treated like one." It's an interesting experience spending time this close to the Hinckley aura. They run a tight ship and their boats are beautiful and well maintained.

Craig and Anne Patterson, friends of the Zinns, invited us aboard *Dream Chaser*, their Hinckley Bermuda Forty. It's a different interior layout than that of *Joye*. It has more open space. I'm still impressed with the dust pan built into the cabin sole that you simply lift out to empty after you have swept the sole. This feature is an example of Hinckley's priority on maintenance, efficiency, and overall attention to detail.

With all the thought about maintenance, it reminded me the time has come to do our boat projects, time to "do the engine," tighten all the nuts, check for leaks of water, diesel, oil, and change or clean all the filters. I spent a happy day crawling in and out of the engine compartment and the lazarette, getting out tools and parts, and in general having lots of boat fun. The rap on the Pearson 323 is that "it takes a skinny contortionist to work on the engine." I am neither a contortionist nor skinny, so I just scrunch and strain to get the job done.

Bezy, meanwhile, took apart the v-berth, removed and cleaned and dried all its nooks and crannies. She wiped off the last of the salt residue that sprayed in through the chain locker, and dried the inside of the hull where water condenses daily because the sea water is colder than the air.

In the afternoon, Nancy and Ron shared with us some of their experience with the Hinckley varnishing team. Hinckley strained the varnish to remove even the smallest particles, and even moved their boat in to the dock so they could vacuum the deck to remove each speck of sanding dust lest it make its way into the finished coat. We joined them at Beal's on the north edge of the harbor for steamed mussels, corn on the cob, wine, and of course, ice cream.

I discovered that the mast step my Florida marina built ten years ago to support the mast is collapsing…slowly. It is a half-inch lower than it was. That explains why we need to tighten the stays a little bit every few weeks. Our designated boat consultant via e-mail from California said, "Your step is only plywood covered over with fiberglass to make it look good."

"Why do you think that?" I asked.

"Because plywood was what was available, lying around the boat yard when they built up the step and glassed it over," he replied.

The Yard manager at Hinckley's was most helpful. "The only material that will withstand the compression load of a mast is polycarbonate (lexan). And, as long as it's only 'sinking slowly,' you ought to be able make it back to Florida before you need to repair it."

The Zinns had a friend with a vacant mooring in Somes Harbor and offered it to us. We decided to sail up Somes Sound, the only fiord in the continental United States, and visit for a day or two. The temperatures were in the 50s at night, and in the 70s, or sometimes creeping just into the 80s in the daytime. On the water, it was usually jacket weather, but jackets were shed quickly as soon as you got on the land. These temperatures were perfect for summer cruising, cool enough that you could snuggle in and get cozy, yet warm enough to go in shirt sleeves ashore.

Before we left Southwest Harbor, we made a last trip ashore to the Maine Point store to buy a new polartec blanket. They make a variety of polartec products for boats, fender covers, pillow slips and blankets. We got one of their blankets six years ago at the Annapolis Boat Show that has kept us warm and snug on very cold nights. Over time it has packed down and needs replacing.

Since we were already there, and as a sense of duty, we walked through West Marine just to make sure there is nothing there that we need to buy. Boaters are like alcoholics when it comes to marine stores, they can't go by one without going in to take a sip. So, true to form, we found something to buy. West had a new head in stock so we bought it. Ours had been giving us trouble and that's one piece of equipment that simply must work.

Leaving our purchases in the stores, we moseyed along Main Street, but when it was time to head back for our trip up Somes Sound, we did so reluctantly because it was an hour before the Ice Cream Shop opened. We tried unsuccessfully for a sneak preview of the mint chocolate chip but to no avail. We gathered the new head and our new blanket and headed back to *Ceilidh*, ready for our next adventure.

The passage up Somes Sound was boating perfection. The crisp Maine sun dressed the trees with its skilled lighting, showing each bough to its best advantage. The sheer rock faces dropped into the water and continued downward, while the rounded cliffs towered skyward. Delectable classic boats, as if especially cast for just such a setting, moved gracefully by. A small schooner was moored, stern to, tied to trees on shore with an anchor off the bow. I expected at any moment to be brought back to reality, but the setting, with its striking beauty, was the reality. As we entered Somes Harbor, the rounded rocks at the water's edge, an orangeish clay color, contrasted with the deep green of the trees making them look even greener. But even that was insufficient preparation for the dramatic impact of a very modern house, built on a huge rock, protruding out over the harbor entrance. The contrast between human construction and nature's extravagance was high drama.

Somes Cove is a thing of beauty. Rock ledges line the shore. Evergreen trees grow in the shallow soil on top of the rock underlayment with one magnificent view after another. The village is little more than a dozen houses lining the state highway, but it is the first settlement on Mount Desert Island, a place founded by a cooper who came from Boston to cut trees and make barrel staves for the whaling ships. We picked up our friend's mooring and settled back to enjoy. Ron and Kathy on *Mooneshine* were moored nearby, so we invited them over for happy hour.

First though, came the day's entertainment, an anchoring dance. A large motor-sailor, anchored to our port, seemed way too close to a dark blue ketch. As I watched, it was clear the motor-sailor was dragging slowly back toward the ketch. No one was in sight on either boat, though the dinghies were both tied astern. Dinghies hanging patiently on their painters are usually evidence that people are aboard. I blew five short blasts...a signal of danger. The two boats came close and almost hit, but at the last minute, the wind shifted slightly, and they eased apart. A man came out on the deck of the ketch and looked around in a casual, unconcerned manner. Then someone appeared in the cabin of the motor-sailor. Its engine throbbed to life. It moved slowly forward and re-anchored. Another crisis averted. I'm not sure whether my intervention helped to precipitate action or was an unwelcome annoyance.

Bezy and Kathy went ashore on a shopping errand to the Port in a Storm bookstore, a unique, well-supplied store with books of sailing and of Maine. Ron and I relaxed in the cockpit, talking about cabin soles and navigating safely in the fog. Since he's sailed a number of years in Maine, I asked him a question I had asked of others.

"How do the lobster boats run at 14 knots in thick fog? Do they have unusually good radars? Or are they especially skilled at seeing in the fog? Are they very knowledgeable of the area? Or are they just confident that other boats will take care of them and get out of the way?"

Ron reported what a lobsterman told him, "We don't go out in the fog. We wonder why boaters 'from away' do."

I knew that was not entirely true since I'd already encountered numerous lobstermen running in thick fog.

The ladies returned, and the four of us enjoyed a pleasant late afternoon visit, talking about boats, family, TV and how much we enjoy not watching it, and the interesting places we have been.

Ron and Kathy initiated "Suddenly Alone Seminars" in the Safety at Sea setting to help couples learn how to take care of each other and handle their boats when one is suddenly ill, or someone goes overboard. Ron's Navy experience and Kathy's professional training in psychology make them uniquely qualified in this area.

The most crucial problem is getting someone back on the boat when they've fallen in the water, especially if the one in the water is the larger, heavier male, and the smaller female is trying to somehow lift or aid him. These are issues all cruisers worry about, and they spend lots of money on equipment in hopes of being prepared. We're never overconfident in this area. We always feel we need more specific training and practice. They invited us over in the morning for an hour-long demonstration of retrieval equipment and its use, a personal mini version of their seminar. After a quick breakfast featuring small, flavorful, local strawberries, we joined Ron and Kathy on *Mooneshine.*

"Man Overboard" is one of the most serious issues of boating. It is even more chilling when there are only two persons on board. The one left on the boat has a number of things to do and they must all be done at once. First, throw a flotation device to the person in the water, a bright yellow "horseshoe" or a floating seat cushion, something to help them float and something that will be more visible than just a human head bobbing in the waves. They must also keep track of where the person overboard is...which is not easy. You're looking for something the size of a cabbage, close to the color of the sea that appears and disappears in 2' to 6' waves. At the same time, they must maneuver the boat back to a position near them. Then they must hold the boat in position while they rig whatever gear they have to help their partner back into the boat. They must assume the person in the water is injured or at least exhausted by his ordeal and can provide little self-help for that will most likely be the case. For most cruisers who are husband/wife teams, it's a one person task, hence the title, "Suddenly Alone."

One lady quipped, "If my husband goes overboard, the only help I'll need is in selling the boat." This commentary was not about her lack of feelings for her husband, but about the extreme, almost impossible difficulty of retrieving someone from the water in rough conditions.

For our training session, Ron and Kathy assumed we had found the person, circled around and drawn them close to the boat with a life sling. They focused on the problems a smaller woman would face raising her larger husband from the water and up onto the deck of the boat. They assumed he was incapacitated and unable to help himself. They had equipment for several approaches to the problem. All involved some kind of lifting rig, a block and tackle attached to a halyard, or a lever device with double cam-cleats that lifted the person in a sling. All had to be rigged quickly and easily. They had to provide significant mechanical advantage, and they had to be able to lift an adult high enough to clear the lifelines and onto the deck. It reminded us again of the urgent need to practice these procedures and to assure that our equipment works, not only on the waters of a calm cove, but on a boisterous ocean with the boat moving erratically. Crises don't happen when the weather is calm with everything happy and easy.

Dock at Southwest Harbor

Chapter 16

To Prospect Harbor

With much to think about, we thanked Kathy and Ron for our special seminar and got underway. We stopped by *Compass Rose* moored nearby to greet Fred and Anne and to meet their son. At the Harbor entrance, we passed yet another Herreshoff twelve-and-a-half. I complimented the captain. "Beautiful boat," I called. The customary response would be something like "Thank you!" and then some comment about your boat. Instead, he answered, "I know! It is indeed." He's right. This little boat is extraordinary and fully justifies the pride their owners take in them.

Just north of Greening Island at the south end of Somes Sound, a couple of Outward Bound boats were making their way slowly toward Southwest Harbor. Outward Bound is a training program in self-reliance and team building for people of all ages. Their students are challenged and develop skills and self-confidence in demanding primitive conditions. For example, in their boating program they use old life boats with a small sail configuration and with oars as auxiliary power. I'm sure their students often feel the oars are the primary power. They camp on shore at night and keep going in whatever the weather offers. Participants learn to work as a team, to appreciate the specific contributions each one makes, and to stretch themselves to do things that take them outside their comfort zone. Bezy attended Outward Bound in the North Carolina mountains where their emphasis was on hiking and camping. It was a significant growth experience for her as she turned fifty. She has great respect and appreciation for the programs. We pulled alongside one of the boats, slowed, and chatted with them briefly as we passed.

A little farther on, a group of Optimist Prams were circumnavigating Greening Island, braving the open water. The young skippers were handling their boats well and seemed to be having a great time. These little 7.5' boats with a sprit rigged sail are ideal to teach sailing. They are stable and dependable. I raced with the first fleet of Opti's in Clearwater, Florida, in 1947 when my dad proposed his idea to the Clearwater Optimist Club. Dad envisioned a small, inexpensive boat sponsored by merchants so that every boy and girl would have a chance to sail. Clark Mills, a local boat builder, created the little gem that has become the largest one-design racing class in the world, sailed in 120 countries on 6 continents. It was gratifying to see the far reaches of Dad's vision and the boys and girls whose lives he had impacted. I couldn't be more proud.

The sky was clear and the clouds white and puffy as we passed through of Northeast Harbor. On our port, the mountains of Mount Desert stretched from the water's edge upward to the sky. It reminded me of Hanamaulu Bay on the island of Kauai in Hawaii. That spectacular bay has low land at the opening then the mountains rise sharply from the sea. The scene is divided by a waterfall cascading down from the high mountain top. My first glimpse of the bay was at dawn after sailing the trade winds through the night from Oahu. The entrance was arched over by a full, brilliant rainbow. Maine has this same kind of spectacular scenery.

As we cleared the protection of Great Cranberry Island, the swells from the open waters of the Atlantic rolled under us. The sea gulls rode the updrafts and soared overhead. With mountains rising from the sea on our left and with nothing but the deep blue ocean on our right, we laid a course across the open water of Frenchman's Bay for the southern tip of Schoodic Island, eight miles away.

The depth sounder registered 5' to 7' of water. That can't be right. The water here is 200' deep. I'm afraid the new depth sounder's transducer is not putting out accurate signals.

The rocks at the tip of Schoodic Island were frothed in foam as the swells coming from thousands of miles across the open ocean crashed against them. The wind built to 20 knots and whitecaps topped the waves. It was a rough crossing and a little bouncy, but *Ceilidh* made her way steadily and easily through the water.

Rounding Schoodic Point, we turned north toward Prospect Harbor...put the waves on our stern and gained an easier ride. The chill, nippy wind felt warmer as we ran with it. We unzipped our jackets.

The two green marks at Prospect Harbor entrance looked innocent enough at high tide and seemed unnecessary. The cruising guides suggest anchoring off the north shore, but the charts indicate rocks in that area. Besides, the water there is jammed with wall-to-wall lobster floats. There was not another sailboat in sight, only the lobster boats moored on the south side of the harbor near a couple of docks and the sardine processing plant.

We anchored just outside the mooring field where we could swing without hitting any of the boats or the trap floats. We dropped a hook and powered back gently to assure it was holding, then dinghied ashore in search of lobsters for dinner. The only place that sold them had a sign, "We're closed today." There were no shops of any kind nor anything else to do ashore. So, after a brief look around, we returned to the boat.

At low tide the rock ledges in mid-harbor and those across the entrance showed themselves as serious hazards. We now understood the value of the green marks and understood their importance even though they were way out at the harbor's edge. Without them marking the safe water, a boat might cut across and get into serious trouble.

We were surrounded by lobster boats, and the humor of the lobstermen showed in their names, *Bug Picker*, and *Fat Bottomed Girl*. Lobstermen call lobsters "bugs." Etymologically lobsters belong to an insect family, hence the name "bugs." About 5 o'clock the next morning, a lobsterman worked a trap within a few feet of our starboard side. I could almost reach across and touch his boat. I'm not sure what he was trying to communicate, or if there was any message at all. He then dropped the trap very close to the boat, so close that as we swung in the wind, the trap line caught on the dinghy motor. It was too close! Lobstermen can be very territorial about their fishing. Maybe he felt the harbor should be reserved for only lobster boats. I was sorry to have disturbed him, but we were planning to leave in a couple of hours anyway.

Prospect Cove lobster boats

Chapter 17

Going "Down East"

The next adventure for the summer was to join my cousin and his family for a few days at Ripley Head. Don't worry if you can't place Ripley Head. Neither can anyone else that's not from this area.

Friends asked, "You're going where?"

"Ripley Head," we said.

"Where is that?"

"It's almost to Roque," we replied.

"Oh!"

They don't know where Roque is either, but at least they've heard of it and know it's an exceptionally beautiful island somewhere out there, near the Canada border. It's not that far, less than 80 miles down the Bold Coast, but for most sailors who are not from Maine, it might as well be in Timbuktu.

"Down East" is what Mainers call the less settled northeastern coast. It is east, and it's down the prevailing wind, hence "down east." It's also called the Bold Coast, bold because it is less inhabited, and bold because of its rugged terrain. Since it is less travelled, there are fewer marks so there are more unidentified ledges of rock ready to take a bite out of your keel...and more challenges in general.

At 8 o'clock, our crew for the day hailed us from the height of the Lobster Coop dock, nearly twenty feet above the water at low tide. They are my cousins from Georgia who have a summer cottage in Ripley Head and have come to provide "pilot" service to guide us between the islands to their place. The three kids clambered down the wooden ladder covered with a thick coat of left-over-bait, algae, and damp sea weed...each one more slippery than the other. I held my breath until they made it safely to the

Small island off Ripley Head

float at the bottom. Their parents, Lucy and John, wisely used the stairs to the side. Lucy Banks, a charming fifteen-year-old, was excited about a chance to sail. She had a sparkle in her eyes and a constant smile across her face to accompany her steady stream of intelligent conversation. McKay was thirteen with both an interest in and a real feel for all things electronic. Andrew was ten, a bit pensive, but one who worked hard to keep up with his older brother and sister, a common trait for a little brother. I know about little brothers; I am one.

Ripley Head had a colony of cottages built around the turn of the century when a return to the rustic life was the rage. A group of cousins got together and built simple cottages close to each other. Lucy's grandfather built one for his family. Most of the cottages have been sold within the family for successive generations. My Georgia-born cousin married into this extended Maine family, having met his wife at the University in Athens. He had to pass the test of love for Maine before his bride agreed to marriage.

The cottages were built of virgin spruce, with no interior siding, no phone, no electricity, and only lately have they added some inside plumbing. A composting toilet is today's most popular approach. Propane gas provides lighting and refrigeration. Propane cooling has now replaced the ice box which was formerly supplied by pond ice, cut in the winter and stored in sawdust pits for summer use. The fireplace, as was the custom in this area of retired sea captains, received special attention. It was paneled with carved boards, often carved by retired ship's carpenters. A cottage industry has built up with the locals helping care for the cottages. Locals living in the area will open and close the cottages for the season, a nice aid for the residents so that the already short summer season is not further shortened by time spent getting the cottage ready.

Sunset off Ripley Head

As we got underway, a fog bank was creeping toward us, but we could still see the harbor entrance. By the time we made it to the green entry marks, however, we were encased in gray. McKay was intrigued with the radar and quickly developed an uncanny sense of what it showed. He helped track its shapes and blips. A few moving blips appeared, boats working nearby, but they approached slowly and remained off to the side. With our eyes, we could see less than an eighth of a mile. All the boats underway appeared to be lobster boats working their traps. None were running at full speed, and there weren't many of them. Everyone was very careful, and there were no near-misses.

Our first GPS waypoint was the western mark of the Petit Manan Bar. The GPS showed its exact position and guided us to it, but we didn't see a thing until we were only three boat lengths off. It gave an eerie moan as we passed. The eastern mark of the bar was just two-tenths of a mile farther, but again we were almost next to it before we caught a glimpse of the tall red floating mark rising and falling easily on the swells.

We steered to two more waypoints before turning up into Pleasant Bay past Flint and Dyer Island without catching a single glimpse of land. We lined up the red nun on the tip of Strout Island with a green can opposite the other end in order to keep in the deep water. We had to accept the radar's report that there were islands just out of sight behind the fog curtain for we saw nothing.

As we were close enough to throw a rock to the shore, the fog began to lift, and we could actually see the Harrington River opening before us.

Lucy said, "Mother will be sure we are still at Prospect Harbor. 'You just can't make it in such weather!' she'd say."

We rounded the north end of Strout, leaving room for the extension of its ledge under the water, but not getting too far off where we might catch the next ledge a little farther on. We attempted to anchor off the rocky beach at Greenwood Cottage, but as we pulled back to set the hook, the kelp interfered and we dragged. Between the known rock bottom and the kelp that readily fouls an anchor, we decided anchoring was not a good idea. John, with foresight, had gotten permission for us to pick up a mooring off the town dock if we needed to. So we moved up the river another quarter mile and moored amidst the lobster boats. We were the only non-working, non-local boat there. It's nice to have local ties on the island at a time such as this.

The mooring pennant was a one-and-a-half inch line that didn't fit under our cleat. It wasn't designed for a boat like ours. I made it work by using a small line to secure it behind the cleat. We were surrounded by fifteen lobster boats and a couple of floats on which they could work their catch. On our stern was a small island, really a large rock, with a one-room house perched on its highest point. As the tide went out, the island trebled in size as the kelp-covered rock uncovered. A brief survey indicated only six of the fifteen lobster boats in the harbor had radars, an interesting statistic as we contemplate joining them out in the fog.

Again the boat names showed humorous irony, *Nap Time,* and *Easy Money.* But my favorite was a rather small boat, almost lost among the others, named *Finally Bigga.*

The launching ramp was busy as men launched small boats to dig clams. Three men in hip boots unloaded thirteen rockers of clams, a good haul. They spent four hours slogging through the mud to find them.

We dinghied ashore, tied to the dock, and were whisked down to Greenwood Cottage and welcomed graciously. After feasting on crab soup, we walked the trails on the point and enjoyed the quiet ambience of the Maine woods. Dinner that night was lobsters, cooked to perfection. The sun, setting over the rocky point and upriver islands, poked through the low-lying clouds to pour itself out on the reflecting waters and turn the sky, water, and rocks a bright red just before the fog began to creep back in. As the sun's glow slowly faded from the rocks, little did we know how long it would be before we'd next see its bright rays.

Grandma Lucy...there are three generations of Lucys here so you need distinctions...with her extensive experience and wisdom, offered us a flashlight for our return to the boat. We politely declined, saying there was usually enough ambient light for us to find our way. She wisely insisted. The only light at the dock was starlight, and with cloud cover, there wasn't any of that. It was not romantic. It was just dark. We really needed the flashlight as we made our way down the dock, untied the dinghy, more feeling than seeing how to proceed. Without the flashlight, we might have fallen off the dock, or have been bumping from one boat to the next trying to find ours as we worked our way through the mooring field.

We were cautioned about the noise of the lobster boats leaving in the morning, but we slept soundly, hardly noticing as they powered up and went out to pull their traps.

Our plan was to take John, Lucy, and the kids sailing, but when we awoke we were still encased in thick fog. We had loaned them our hand-held radio and thus were able to communicate and develop alternate plans. John suggested a drive up the coast to the St. Croix River, cross into Canada and go down the Canadian side to St. Andrews for lunch. At a roadside stand along the way we found the first of this year's crop of wild Maine blueberries, the tiny tasty ones. We also bought pies and pastries for the one-hundred-year celebration at the cottage on Saturday. As we traveled, Grandma Lucy regaled us with her experiences as a child and pointed out this and that aunt's home as we passed. Her roots run deep and are planted widely over the area. A bronze plaque, fastened to a granite monument, marked the 45th parallel of latitude, half-way between the equator and the North Pole. We paused to note the passage. It feels like we're much farther north than just halfway. It's interesting how perceptions need to be adjusted to reality.

Canada had a neatly clipped, flowered face. Its people smiled easily. Grandma Lucy treated us to lunch at a garden cafe in St. Andrew before our return trip. On the way back, we took a highway that follows a ridge through the middle of the state. Mountainous inland Maine is as spectacular in its own way as is the coast, I'm told. We could see very little because of the continuing fog. We were disappointed not to see a moose standing beside the road to greet us. From the tourist information we'd read, we were led to expect one on every corner.

After dinner in Machias and a walk through the gallery of an artist's colony, a tired, sleepy group returned home. It was a most interesting day on the land, an unusual treat for boaters whose usual range is a mile or so hike inland from the coast.

As we awoke, the fog had retreated eastward toward the Gulf of Maine. We decided to try to sail, despite the light wind and the hazy cloud cover. We boarded six passengers and got underway. The breeze filled to 8 knots as we tacked out Pleasant Bay. John, Lucy, and the children were viewing their islands from a different perspective, from the water rather than the land. They enjoyed trying to identify the islands and familiar points of interest. McKay and Andrew handled the jib as we tacked, wrapping the sheet around the self-tailing winch and cranking it in. When the fog headed back inshore, Bezy served hot chocolate and dug out coats and jackets while the cool, damp breeze chilled us to the bone. So much for sailing. We furled the sails and returned to our mooring.

That evening, we were guests of a cousin at Dixie Cottage, Grandma Lucy's parents' home. She told the tale of when she was four and the lobsters got loose in the kitchen. Her parents were away, and she was there alone with their cook, Tilley, whom the family brought with them from Georgia. Tilley opened the door and discovered the lobsters crawling about on the kitchen floor. She was scared to death. Lobsters were foreign to her Georgia experience. But she had a duty to do, so putting aside her fear, she courageously cared for her small charges. She hurriedly closed all the doors to the kitchen, and covered the children and herself with her apron in the farthest corner of the cottage until the parents returned.

Liles and Michael, our hosts, provided roasted Georgia pecans and a crab spread, accompanied by stories and tales of the relatives who had lived there in the past. Michael is Sculptor-in-Residence at Georgia State University in Atlanta. He spends his summers in Maine searching for hidden likenesses of fish and animals in dead stumps, branches and limbs. He taught McKay and Andrew to create art from the driftwood they found on the shore. "Little Lucy", the fifteen-year-old, under his tutelage, dried and flattened birch bark for the place cards for the dinner table.

Today everyone is busy preparing for the 100th year celebration of Greenwood, the Nickerson, Tresp, Sheftal Cottage, named for all the families that have owned it in recent years. We're invited. But, since we're not needed for preparations, they loaned us a car to do our washing in nearby Columbia Falls.

The Scrub It Laundromat's clientele is varied and diverse, as evidenced by the car license plates from Florida, Georgia, New Jersey, Nevada, Virginia, Mexico, and a couple even from Maine. Mexicans are here as farm workers to rake Maine blueberries. A sign on the window of Scrub It, advertises Help Wanted for additional workers to rake. We're tempted to give it a try. It would be an interesting experience, but I know my back wouldn't last 20 minutes.

The rain, that had been with us all morning, stopped just long enough for us to return the dry clothes to the boat before heading back to Greenwood Cottage and the big celebration

The 100th Anniversary party for Greenwood Cottage was festive. Sixteen people were seated for dinner, illumined with intimate gas lights and candles. The dining room of the cottage is an add-on, a former doll house of another cottage that was moved in place and connected. It couldn't hold the crowd, so two card tables were set in the living room for the overflow. The children helped serve. The Maine shrimp Newburg was delicious as was the home-baked pie a la mode. Conversations around the table ranged from the current political and world situation, to local island politics, and to the racial integration of the Universities of Georgia and Mississippi in the 60s. Lothar was a faculty member at University of Georgia while I was University Pastor at Ole Miss during those years. We discussed some topics from medieval times and an interesting treatise by Farley Mowatt about the tribes who were pushed out of Scotland, built skin-covered boats, and cruised the islands of the North Atlantic as far west as Newfoundland, harvesting Walrus tusks. The conversation ranged far and wide, but inevitably returned to the history and the families of Ripley Head.

With hugs all around, we said our goodbyes and headed back to *Ceilidh* with a delightful taste of what life had been like in these parts for more than a century. We also took with us a distinctive contemporary experience of the warmth and graciousness of our cousins, their family, and friends.

Sunset through the fog

Chapter 18

Further "Down East"

It was time to leave Ripley Head and head to Roque, but the fog continued to blanket us as it had for the last three days. The passage going farther east from here is not as straightforward or as well marked as the waters through which we have come. If we could take the passage inland through the Moosabec Thoroughfare past Jonesport, we would have the advantage of more marks, and we would be inshore where the fog would not affect us as much. However, our mast is taller than the 39' clearance of the bridge, so we have to go outside, around Great Wass and Steele Harbor Islands where the marks are infrequent and where there is an indistinct passage through unmarked ledges when you finally make your turn north toward Roque. We'd love to visit Roque Island, but it's a hard decision to venture forth into this scantly marked area with limited visibility. The forecast called for fog, rain, more

Ripley Harbor in the fog

fog and thundershowers in the days ahead. Bezy's stomach was a tad off, so we decided to stay put and take it easy on the boat. The fog stayed put too.

At five o'clock, John called. He had driven down to the dock and noted we were still on the mooring. We hadn't left as we had planned. He invited us to join them for lobster dinner on the beach. I went, but Bezy wasn't up to standing around or to sitting on the hard rocks. The whole crew from the cottages gathered, including a number of uninvited mosquitoes. Malcolm boiled a pot of lobsters over a wood fire nestled between the rocks. Tank roasted some fresh cod he had just caught. Michael prepared blueberry crepes in a frying pan as the driftwood fire burned down to glowing embers, just right for crepes. Liles provided home baked cookies. It was a New England clambake, or more precisely a Maine lobster boil at its finest. They sent a lobster home with me for Bezy. We had another round of goodbyes and hugs, and asked ourselves, "What can we do to thank these people for their wonderful hospitality? The best thing we can do is to leave, just leave." This was the punch line from a similar experience in Pensacola, Florida where friends had been so gracious to us for several days. It was once again applicable. It is time to leave, but...

The weather continues with its gray moist fuzzes, and the forecast for the week doesn't project any change. Fog and more fog. Bezy quoted Grandma's saying to the weatherman... "If you can't say something nice, don't say anything at all," as she swatted the radio's off button...with emphasis. It may be time to leave, but it's certainly not prudent to do so. We'll just have to wait a little longer.

We needed to cut hair. It was long, long overdue. So we dinghied ashore and perched on the granite wall of the dock and began to snip. We've been cutting each other's hair for eight years now. It's so much easier than all the trouble of trying to find someone ashore to do it. Then when you locate a hair dresser or barber, you have to figure out how to get there. The fog was so thick it wet our hair instantly...no need for a preparatory shampoo to hold the hair and make it easier to trim. A "lobster lass," one of the new breed of women who are going lobstering, came up from the dock, an attractive blonde, about thirty years of age. She was enthusiastic about her work, happy to be her own boss despite the challenges and physical demands of working a lobster boat. After chatting a minute, we asked her to take our picture with the boats in the background, recording this historic hair-fog moment on film.

Bezy shared her lobster from the previous night, and we had lobster rolls for lunch. A glass of white wine was a perfect complement. We'll show the fog it can't get us down. As the rain, fog, and darkness settled, we listened to Offenbach and Bizet, courtesy of modern day electronics, compact enough for a small boat. We watched a DVD of *City Slickers* in the improbable setting of down east Maine, in pitch dark, on a boat. Yee Ha! Thank God for microchips and transistors and for all the other amazing miniaturized electronics that are available. We spent another night wrapped in the muffled silence of fog.

The weatherman forecasts more rain, fog, and cold. A pox on the weatherman and his weather. But he's only the messenger and you're not supposed to shoot the messenger. We can't see the other side of the river, much less all the way out to the islands. We can't go anywhere. Not today. Not in the foreseeable future. But we can make a decision. We decided not to risk getting stuck at Roque in the fog. We've changed our plans. We'll head for Winter Harbor or Sorrento back to the west when it is feasible to go, but it's far from clear when that might be.

The sea gulls stood stolidly on the rocks, each on a separate rock, all facing into the wind, like a sullen choir awaiting the conductor's baton and silently hoping he doesn't show. The wet and fog have silenced their squawking and fussing. The scene of wet grumpy birds brought back the pictures of the birds standing soaked and desolate on the Tempelhof Airport runways in Berlin during the Berlin Airlift. The planes to supply the city were landing every minute in weather too nasty for even the birds to fly.

Meanwhile, on board *Ceilidh*, we read, wrote on the computer and caught up on our rest. We had plenty of food, good supplies of diesel, water and propane. All that we were running out of was patience, but we worked hard, in a vain attempt, to replenish that and in general were quite unsuccessful.

Meanwhile, our lobstermen neighbors disappeared each morning into the fog and returned later with their catch. There was plenty of activity and sometimes significant wakes as they moved about. So much for the lobsterman's comment quoted to us that unlike the crazy cruisers, lobstermen didn't go out in the fog. Here, the lobstermen were going out, and the cruiser was staying put.

Fog not only inhibits movement and creates additional hazards, but it also steals the beauty of the Maine coastline, or at least masks it in a dull misty gray. There's a certain ghostly beauty of a boat isolated by the fog, hanging on its anchor, its reflection showing in the still water. But this scene isn't nearly as attractive when it's viewed from the boat at anchor...from the inside...looking out the ports...for the fourth day in a row. It rained several times during the night. Does rain wash away the fog? Nope! It's still foggy.

Fog, fog, and more fog. We were hearing a broken record. We caught the TV "nightly mayhem report" as we usually call what masquerades as "nightly news." The weather radar showed clouds and rain streaming up the entire east coast of the United States with no sign of a break anytime soon. We may have to make a run for it. But not today. We can't even see the dock on the shore, and it's less than 30 yards off. It's time to bake banana bread and to search for some other "rainy day in the fog" activity.

Rich Payne called on the phone and asked about meeting us somewhere in a couple of days. He plans to drive up from Annapolis, "for a little break." I hope he's been checking the weather reports of Maine and understands what kind of "break" he'll be getting. He said there was warm rain falling in the Chesapeake. He knows about cruising and how it works. He can be flexible. He will adjust to wherever we are and meet us there. We look forward to seeing him, maybe in Bar Harbor in a few days.

Today the weatherman called for visibility of one nautical mile, increasing to one to three in the afternoon. I'm not sure I believe him, but he's forecasting nothing better for the next week. The extended forecast calls for rain, thunderstorms, fog, and yet more rain. A high pressure system, far out on the Atlantic, has locked the jet stream in a trough that dips to Georgia and runs up the entire east coast. There's a train of lows bringing "trainloads" of moisture to Maine. A state official declared the drought of the last couple of years to be officially over. With all the moisture we've had, we can certainly believe that.

It looked like the thing to do was to go ahead and go. A mile's visibility is not great, but it's certainly workable. We could pick up buoys visually as well as on GPS and Radar, and a mile was more than enough to avoid another boat running into us. We had just been through the area ten days ago, so we were somewhat familiar with it. It was time to go.

We planned our strategy carefully, using the many navigational tools we had. We hoped for a break in the fog, but didn't count on it. Assuming that the heat of the sun would lessen or lift the fog, we waited until 10:30 to leave for our 25-mile passage to Winter Harbor. We started out slowly, dodging the many lobster traps in the river, waving to the lobstermen we'd been cloistered with this last week. They emerged from the fog, then disappeared again, working their trap. It was hard to know whether they admire our courage for pressing on or clucked at our foolishness. We were not sure ourselves.

The next hurdle was an unmarked ledge just north of Strout Island. It should be visible at this tide, and our trackback on the GPS will lead us back the way we came. Our instruments guided us past the ledge, but we saw it only when we were almost on it, about twenty yards to our port. Radar indicated the boats working around us, but we saw only their vague outlines as we passed. We saw the other islands on radar, but Strout is the only one we actually saw with our eyes, about 70 yards to port. The red can on its south end was the beginning of our entry to wider water and fewer traps. Navigation was easier from there on. It was time to take a couple of deep breaths. We weren't aware that we had been breathing so hesitantly.

The weatherman missed his projection by three-quarters of a mile. He said "a mile's visibility," but we never saw more than one-quarter of a mile, and most of the time it was only one tenth. And his forecast for the afternoon, "one to three miles," was fiction. However, we did okay with the limited visibility we had. We made our way from waypoint to waypoint guided by the GPS. The radar showed no other boats moving. Occasionally, we picked up a lobster boat as a blip a half mile off, usually holding in place outside a buoy, but we didn't actually see any of them. We identified a buoy off Dyer Island on the GPS and on the radar, but it was a tenth of a mile away when we first saw it, and then only as a dark shadow through the thick fog.

We also had to keep watch on the water for the lobster pots. We snagged a line of one. It caught briefly on the keel, and then slid off and under the rudder and floated free. It was the small light tan toggle attached to the main float. Almost every float has such a secondary float called a toggle. The major float leads directly to the trap while the toggle drifts off down wind or down current, close to the surface. If you pass between the two floats, you can snag the toggle line on your keel, rudder or prop. We lucked out this time, but we need to watch more carefully in the future.

The day had another "gotcha." For the first time, the rockweed floating on the surface was thick enough and hung deep enough to catch on the prop. We caught it a couple of times. Each time it happened, we slowed, shifted into reverse and were able to throw most of it off. I got the last little bit off later at anchor by slowly rotating the prop by hand and wiggling it a bit when each blade pointed down, allowing the rockweed to fall off.

I was anxious about passing over the Petit Manan Bar since we would arrive at dead low tide with a four-foot swell. The swell was slightly reduced on the bar, but the depth sounder showed only 13' of water. If the trough between the swells dropped us down on the rock it would be quite a jolt. It was a significant relief when the second buoy on the east side of the bar loomed up ahead of us and the depth began to rise...16'...21'...25.'

We had a good echo of Schoodic Island on the radar screen. We rounded the number two nun off the tip of the island and headed up the bay toward Turtle Island. As we turned, the wind was from a new direction. The mist blew into our faces, wet our clothes, and coated our glasses. It took constant wiping, back and forth, back and forth, like windshield wipers. Only our glasses were not equipped with wipers and we had to use paper towels...and they had to be operated by hand...back and forth...back and forth.

We hoped the fog would clear as we entered Winter Harbor with the land in close on both sides, but it persisted. We could see land on one shore if we favored it, but only one shore at a time. We held to port and entered Sand Cove, by the Winter Harbor Yacht Club. Half a dozen classic yachts were on moorings nearby as we anchored in thirty-five feet of water.

It was a demanding trip in the fog, but one that was rather straightforward with all the tools we had available...auto-helm...depth sounder...radar...trackback line on GPS...good charts...and a reliable compass. We used all of these carefully and in concert. We had more information than we needed and knew where we were at all times. There was no problem detecting the boats moving around us, and we were never in any danger. But four-and-a-half hours of such eye popping, concentration kept us on edge. A hot cup of tea was more than welcome as we ducked below, took off our raingear, and settled in for the night. Even in this protected anchorage at the head of the bay, we felt some movement from the ocean swells, but not enough to keep us awake, not tonight.

The Bangor newscasters were on the case of their weatherman when he called for continued rain and fog. But he did offer a bit of hope for next weekend, that's right, NEXT weekend. That seems a long time off, too long. It was time for better weather, but it seemed we would just have to wait a little longer.

Chapter 19

Back from the Bold Coast

Finally, we were back from the Bold Coast. There were times when we wondered if we'd ever make it back. The fog and the rain seemed prepared to hang around until fall, or even winter. With the cold wet weather we've had, it seems ironic that our first anchorage "back west" was named <u>Winter</u> Harbor. It appeared to be a pleasant harbor, and despite the fact we haven't been ashore to explore, we decided to move on to Bar Harbor for a little more activity, a meal out, and other land experiences.

A gentle rain continued, but the wind was from the northeast which might indicate an approaching high pressure and the clearing that would accompany it. The cove was clear of fog. Maybe, just maybe, or was that too much to expect, we might be able to see where we were going? We retrieved 125 feet of anchor chain and headed out.

The entire length of Winter Harbor was visible all the way down to the point. We could see Turtle Island's red nun buoy as we rounded Mark Island and turned up into Friendship Bay. Egg Rock lighthouse was wearing a thin fog tutu around its waist. Wisps of fog lingered. We did a "do-si-do" with a lobster boat as we attempted to dodge the boat, the many floats it was working, and a large bell buoy all at the same time. But we could see! We could see!

This morning I discovered something new, a new way to avoid lobster traps. There were no traps in the deep water approach to Bald Porcupine Island. If you always run in water 250 feet deep, you avoid the traps. It was not a very practical solution. Deep water was not easy to find. But at least that's one way to avoid the pesky game of "dodge the floats."

Just as we congratulated ourselves on good visibility and the absence of lobster buoys, there was a serious sounding "clunk." There was only one clunk, and the engine didn't slow. We were in 260' of water so we didn't clip a ledge. It was obvious something happened under the boat, but what? What made the "clunk?" Unexplained "clunks" are not acceptable on a boat. Looking aft, there was a medium-size board that floated up to the surface. It appeared to have been split. Evidently the "clunk" was when we broke the board with our prop. There was no vibration, so the prop wasn't bent. It seemed that all was well! Maybe "Murphy" thought, without the excitement of fog, we needed a little excitement of a different kind.

The fog was patchy and seemed to be playing hide-and-seek with the islands. There was a wisp here, another there. A gray band of thin fog lay around an island to our right. The treetops were covered here and there. The scene changed every minute. It was wispy, light, playful fog.

The Porcupines, islands that surround Bar Harbor, are stark rock islands with pointed trees on top. They get their name from their wintertime dress when the bare pointed tree trunks look for all the world like porcupine quills. Burnt Porcupine, to the northeast, had a thin veil of cloud drawn across it. It looked like the island's treetops were peeping seductively over a veil shading its face.

A Harbor Cruise passed us. They were outbound with a dozen passengers who seemed to be caught up by the sullen weather and had become sullen themselves. They didn't even bother to return our wave. I imagine the tourist industry is seriously hurting with the nasty weather we've been having and the effect it's having on everyone's mood.

On the outer edge of the harbor, five kayakers called a "Securite...Securite" on VHF Channel 16, "For all concerned traffic..." They were crossing the harbor in the fog and called on the radio to make other boats aware they were there so the larger, faster powered boats would be on the lookout for the small, low profile kayaks.

The cruising guide indicated depths of seven to seventy-eight feet in the anchorage. That's a surprisingly large range. As we slowly circled, looking for a place to anchor, we passed a couple of very large yachts anchored in seventy-eight feet of water. We were not interested in putting out or pulling in that much chain. So, after a couple of turns through the area without locating a suitable spot in shallow water, we decided not to anchor and to pick up a mooring instead.

Bar Harbor is not completely enclosed. It is protected by several islands, Bar Island, the Porcupines, and two others. There are connections between most of them. There is an extensive gravel bar that connects Bar Island to Mount Desert, but only when the tide goes out and it uncovers. For part of the day at least, you can drive or walk across to the island. Because of this access, it is a popular tourist spot. One night we heard bagpipes, and being of Scottish heritage we went on deck to listen. A piper serenaded us for an hour as the tide slowly rose to where he stood. He stopped playing and left just as the rising tide covered the gravel bar.

To the south, Bald Porcupine is connected to Mount Desert with a man-made granite breakwater. Through the years, the waves have beat on it and broken it down. At each high tide, there was a three-hour period during which the ocean swells came over the top and surged across the harbor. The swells were unimpeded from the Falkland Islands, or whatever land lies between Maine and Antarctica to the south. At each high tide, we experienced a new meaning for the term "rock and roll."

The harbor was busy with lobster boats, tour boats of all sizes, and ferries on their regular runs to nearby islands. A few small local sailboats were moored near us next to the harbor's eighteen transient moorings. With the exposed sea conditions and a very congested harbor, not many cruising boats make extended stays here despite the interesting possibilities ashore.

For the first few days, the fog came and went, sometimes blanketing us, other times leaving only ribbons across the distant islands. But when the fog returned in full force, we could scarcely see the boats only a few feet away. One foggy night, when we returned to the boat after dark, it was a bit chancy to find *Ceilidh*. We found her only because we had left a trail of lobster shells, the water version of bread crumbs, on the water to guide us back. Actually, we entered a way point for our moored boat and used our handheld GPS to guide us.

The dinghy dock where all the dinghies of the moored boats were tied, was a long dock with an extra float on the end that the lobstermen use to take on supplies and off-load their catch. It lay alongside the high granite block wall of the wharf and was reached by slanting stairs that adjusted to the ever-changing height of the tide. The long dock was chock full of wooden and fiberglass rowboats that took up considerable space and made it difficult to find a place to tie up. In addition, at high tide, the massive chains that attached the dock to the wharf were only a couple of feet off the water. To get under them and access the back side of the dock, you had to scrunch down into the dinghy and squeeze under. If the tide was very high and the chains too low, you couldn't get under at all and had to go to the far end and negotiate between the boats and the high granite wall until you could find a place, push the boats apart, and squeeze in. It was much easier to find a place in the morning when the lobstermen were out and their rowboats were tied to the moorings out in the harbor. Late afternoons and evenings it was a real bear to find any room at the dock at all.

Bar Harbor had a variety of shops, curio shops, specialty shops with high tech climbing and hiking gear, boating supplies, a balsamic vinegar shop, T-shirts and moose logo shops, and a very special place that offers the works of local artists. Our shopping needs were very specific. We needed only the essentials: a laundromat, a grocery store, a library, an internet café, a place to buy cooked lobster, and the local Chamber of Commerce for information about all the special activities during the time we were here.

Rich, a long time cruising friend, arrived from Annapolis. He brought his handheld VHF radio and hailed us from the wharf. We dinghied in to pick him up, and while we were there, got steamed lobsters to take back to the boat for dinner. Since we can't keep ice cream on the boat, we had to go back ashore and finish the meal with Bar Harbor's finest blueberry ice cream. For some reason, it tasted unusually good that night. It took several hours of chatting and catching up to cover all that had happened since we were last together.

We decided not to go for a sail down Frenchman's Bay since the weather was still wet and foggy. Instead, we headed inland by car to Ellsworth to attend church. We arrived at the Congregational Church at eleven o'clock. Two ushers were standing in the back with the offering plates, so we slipped past them and into a nearby pew as the choir finished their anthem. After the offering was received, the minister announced the closing hymn. Oops! The traditional hour for morning worship at this church was not 11:00 as we assumed. We'd goofed. We laughed at ourselves, and the amused parishioners suppressed their chuckles as we left.

Ellsworth was much larger than we expected. We checked out Reny's, a local discount store that we'd heard of and wanted to see what they carried and whether they had things boat people needed. We shopped at Walmart for a couple of things, and of course stopped by the L.L.Bean factory store, a must for our dedicated L.L.Bean shopper, Bezy. A roadside stand had local Maine blueberries for $3 a quart. Sadly we can utilize only one quart at this point, and when we'll be ready for more, we'll be on the water, unable to get them. Rich treated us to a lobster dinner at a roadside restaurant just near the airport. While we were eating, the clouds were blown away and the sun emerged, at least that's what that grand yellow ball in the sky was called, to the best of my memory.

Rich drove us on an auto tour of Acadia National Park, down around the point to Sand Beach, past Jordan Pond and Eagle Lake, and up to the top of Cadillac Mountain. As we drove through the wooded sections of the park, I was unprepared for the beauty of the sunlight filtering down through the oak, maple, and birch trees, leaving bright patches of sunlight on the roadway and the forest floor. The overpasses were carefully marked with red granite blocks, hewn from nearby quarries. From the top of the mountain, we gazed across Frenchman's Bay to the distant islands and named the ones we'd anchored beside. Looking down on the harbor, we saw *Ceilidh* hanging on her mooring and the white dots that were small boats, their sails catching the afternoon breeze. Shortly after we reached the top of the mountain, however, the day began to cool and the clouds returned. Soon the mountain was covered with mist, and we could see only 50 yards down the sloping side. The views we'd enjoyed disappeared. Instead of the islands, we saw the top of a layer of clouds, much like what you see from any high flying plane.

We drove down the mountain through the clouds and returned to Bar Harbor and out across the gravel bar to Bar Island at the north end of the harbor. The roadway was wide and firm despite the fact that it spent more than half of each day underwater, a most interesting phenomenon.

As we shared all our fog experiences with Rich, he added a new oddity from his cruise on his sloop *Odyssey*. He had noted a blip on radar which appeared stationary. The chart showed no mark in the area. It could be an anchored boat or disabled boat, or something drifting. He approached the blip cautiously but all he saw was a large flock of puffins floating on the water. How could small birds reflect a radar signal? Then he noticed metal marking bands on their legs. All of them were wearing them. Evidently the metal bands of all the birds clustered together were enough to reflect the radar signal. It takes a lifetime of experience to not be surprised by radar.

Since we were where we could get water at any time, we allowed our third water tank to run out, to see how long our water supply would last. We kept the water jugs for drinking filled, to avoid any serious inconvenience. Being careful, we managed to make our eighty-gallon supply last twenty-six days. The last tank went dry as Bezy was washing the dinner dishes on the twenty-sixth day. Next morning, I shaved with the boiling water left from making the morning tea. Bezy washed her face, wet her hair, and brushed her teeth with a chilled bottle of drinking water. We learned long ago to not let the water run while you brush your teeth or when you shave. When you shower, you wet down, turn off the water and soap up, and then turn the water back on for a brief rinse. We really used very little water. Ashore, with an unlimited supply, most people use much more than is necessary.

The fuel dock was a finger dock with space on both sides. It was occupied by two large cruise boats. We observed the times they were away from the dock and timed our move to go in and take on fuel and water while they were away. We edged alongside, topped off the diesel, and filled our water tanks. The fuel dock is nestled close between the town dock and another dock designed for a two-hundred-foot whale watching craft. It was easy to get in, but a bit of a trick to get out. We used the ancient method of warping. Attach a line, known as a warp, to the dock then back down on it and it leverages the boat, pivoting it around. This procedure was used to turn the great sailing ships, work them off the dock, and point them out to sea.

About noon, our daughter Heidi and grandson Jackson arrived by plane at the Bar Harbor airport. The plane, the terminal, and the number of passengers were all downsized to fit a small seasonal tourist destination. We took the Island Explorer out to meet them and returned an hour later on the next bus. The bus is operated by the National Park Service with some local financial help. The propane-powered buses follow eight routes around the park, campgrounds, hotels and popular park locations. They save on emissions, wear and tear on the roads, and ease the parking and driving congestion. We used it extensively during our time in and around the park.

We loaded the baggage and the four of us into *Wee Ceilidh*, our nine-foot inflatable dinghy and went out to the boat. With this many people, we had to sit on the side tubes with our feet in the boat. "Remember to lean in," I cautioned, "and, no back flips overboard." Visitors to a boat should bring a very limited amount of luggage, only the absolute essentials. Heidi and Jackson had been aboard before and were experienced and thoughtful boat visitors.

While Bezy welcomed them and got them settled onboard, I dinghied back to the Island Fisherman dock, selected four shedder lobsters and waited while they were boiled. For dinner, we feasted on the delight of Maine. I was surprised to learn that lobster had not always been prized as a delicacy. Native Americans did not eat them at all, nor did the early settlers. At that time, lobsters were used to fertilize the crops. They were so plentiful you could reach into the shallow water and pick them up with your bare hands, no need for boats or traps. Island children who brought lobster sandwiches for their lunch were identified as "poor." People of means just didn't eat such things. It was only in this century that lobsters came to be valued as a fine delicacy. They are messy as you crack open the shells and dig out the meat, but the taste is tender and succulent once you get to the pink, soft flesh in the tail and the claws. Neptune, the god of the sea, honored our guests and kept things calm during high tide that night so we could all sleep soundly.

The morning dawned bright and clear. Heidi and Jackson must have brought the good weather with them from Tennessee. We, and the rest of the tourists who had come to Maine for its cool brisk sunny weather, were ecstatic. During breakfast in the cockpit, a huge cruise ship peeked around the end of Bald Porcupine Island and eased gingerly into the harbor. The *Serenade of the Seas*, sent her passengers ashore in small launches to tour the island and to do some shopping. We joined the crowd. We took the Oli Trolly tour of the Acadia Park which included the view from atop Cadillac Mountain. From the mountain top, on a clear day like today, we could see both inland and far out to sea. We continued to identify islands, a project that had been interrupted the other day when the clouds rolled in. The trolley was entirely open on the sides, so as we rode, we felt the cool breeze, smelled the trees and the surf, and embraced Acadia with all five senses.

Lobster Trap Float

The next day, after one day of glorious sunshine, we awoke to fog. But it didn't seem like the kind of fog that would hang around all day. The air wasn't saturated enough to support fog, and it was warm. Maybe the fog would burn off as the sun rose in the sky. It did. We packed a picnic lunch and took the Island Explorer to Somesville to see the children's play, *The Wind in the Willows*, by Kenneth Grahame, featuring everyone's favorite characters, Toad, Rattie, Mr. Beaver, Mole and Mrs. Otter. We selected seats on the second row behind an experienced, clever, grandfather who spent the time waiting for the play to start, making up a story with his grandchildren, seven and nine years of age. Seemingly, such stories were their usual custom while they waited. The children chose the setting, a boat, a picnic, a downtown street, a circus. The story then featured an adventuresome pair of children named Snigglefritz and Daisy Mae. Grandpa and grandchildren created the story together.

"Where would you like to go today?" asked Grandpa.

"I want to go to a circus," said Snigglefritz.

We eavesdropped shamelessly as Grandpa told how Snigglefritz, with no fear, calmly picked up a chair and worked the escaped circus lion back into his cage. Meanwhile, Daisy Mae slipped into a flyer's costume and mounted the trapeze.

"What stunts are you planning?" Grandfather asked.

"I think I'll do a double flip and then drop gracefully from the trapeze into the safety net," answered a confident Daisy Mae.

Grandfather cupped his hands and announced, "Ladies annnnnnnd gentlemen, give your attention to the center ring where the amaaaaazzzzzzing Miss Daisy Mae will perform the death defying double flip on the trapeze."

Daisy Mae climbed up the precarious ladder to the platform high up in the tent. She swung out and back, and then let go of the bar and flipped gracefully into the hands of the catcher. After another swing he released her and she dropped to the safety net. She bounced up, arms outstretched to receive the applause for her feat.

This creative grandfather was such a good storyteller that we almost burst into applause, thinking we were actually at the circus.

When the play started, Toad squatted and leapt around the stage with the easy rhythm of a frog. Beaver's moves by contrast were heavy and sullen. The actors drew us in to the life of the animals. The play was skillfully performed with either professional actors or very talented college level performers. Afterwards, when Toad greeted his young audience and signed autographs, he remained in character, crouching and leaping about from time to time. The kids were spellbound. So were us older kids when Rat delivered the classic line that explains the passion of boaters in a single sentence, "There's nothing, absolutely nothing so much worth doing as messing, simply messing about in boats."

The play over, we walked up the road to Somes Harbor to enjoy a picnic in the shade of the trees while we checked the harbor to see if we recognized any of the boats anchored there. We found a few rocks to sit on, and the cool breeze made for a fine picnic.

Bar Harbor from Mt. Desert

We next ventured south on the Island Explorer, to Southwest Harbor for a look-see at the shops there. Heidi found a pillow filled with balsam needles, like the one we had on the boat. With the pillow, she would capture a fragrance of Maine and take it back home to Tennessee. After an hour's wandering and a dollop of ice cream, we caught the return bus for Bar Harbor and the boat.

After a leisurely start with tea and cereal in the cockpit, we went to the Ivy Manor Inn for brunch to celebrate my birthday. The chef explained the specialties of the day, bacon cooked with brown sugar and pecan chips, mussels, baked salmon and blueberry pancakes. We ate under the trees on the outside porch with a cool breeze blowing. Blueberry pancakes made with small wild Maine blueberries make a fine birthday cake. With a birthday in mid August, a traditional vacation month, I've celebrated in many different places and situations. This was one of the finest.

After lunch, we worked off our meal on the walk along the ocean in front of the older cottages. This seaside walk has been maintained by the property owners as a gift to the public so everyone could enjoy the rocky shore and the view of tides washing up and back. Theirs is a distinctive approach to waterfront property, sharing rather than blocking it off and attempting to keep others away.

John D. Rockefeller looked far ahead when he envisioned the national park of Acadia, and donated property for it. The park was first known as Lafayette National Park. Rockefeller planned and built a road for cars around the perimeter of the island, and then built sixty-seven miles of carriage roads inside that outer circle. The carriage roads were restricted to horse-drawn carriages, cyclists and hikers. At the time, cars were just coming into vogue and carriages were on the way out. Rockefeller's vision carried far into the future and has provided an excellent usage of the space of this rare natural resource into the twenty first century. What we'd already seen of the park was so intriguing that we made reservations for a carriage ride around Day Mountain.

Next day, the Island Explorer dropped us off at the Wildwood Stables for our ride. The driver, a retired lawyer from Louisville, Kentucky, was the head of the stables and the entire carriage program. He began as a volunteer, but enjoyed that so much that he retired early and moved here to work fulltime. Heidi and Jackson sat on the seat beside him and helped direct the horses. The slow pace of the carriage, stopping every now and then to let the horses rest after a strenuous climb uphill, was just right. It allowed us time to absorb and savor the woods and the views. It reminded us of our leisurely pace on the boat and all the extra that the relaxed pace allows us to do and see, things we would miss if we weren't moving slowly on a sailboat, on the water.

On this excursion, we learned that the great fire that devastated the island of Mount Desert in 1947, began in the town dump at Hull Cove on the northwestern edge of the island. Following a drought, the trees were dry tinder, and when a seventy-knot wind pushed the fire across the island at devastating speed, it burned everything in its path, stopping only at the water's edge. All anyone could do was to dash to the nearest boat and escape on the water. Surprisingly, only two people were killed. For some reason which no one could explain, the spruce, pine and balsam fir trees were replaced by oak, maple and birch when the forest was replanted, changing significantly the character of the woods.

On a special carriage ride that our driver took with his four-year-old daughter, she asked, "Did Mr. Rockefeller build the Island?"

"No, Amy," her father responded, "God built the Island. Mr. Rockefeller just built the roads."

Amy pondered a moment and then responded, "Well, they both did good work."

As if our carriage ride wasn't enough fun for one day, at its conclusion, we took the bus to the Jordan Pond Restaurant for afternoon Tea and Popovers, like the rich and famous did years before. The restaurant has been a fixture at the south end of Jordan Pond for a long time. The pond was also the beginning point of many walking and cycling trails for this section of the park.

We were interested to have the traditional popovers, but had no idea what a "popover" was. Everyone spoke well of them, so we figured they must be good. They arrived at our table golden brown and hot from the oven, looking like oversized muffins or a miniature pastry version of a chef's hat. When we broke them open, they were hollow inside, making a hot, light, egg bread cup that held lots of butter and strawberry jam. It was a perfect conclusion to a throwback day from years gone by.

Heidi and Jackson took a walking tour of town, visited the whale museum and the Indian museum, and walked across the bar to Bar Island, while Bezy and I tended to a bit of washing, grocery shopping, and a visit to the Internet Cafe to send e-mail.

Back at the wharf we overheard talk of a lobsterman taking out a couple of visitors to pull lobster traps in the fog. The visitors asked, "How did you find that lobster trap in the fog?"

"I put it there, so I knew where it was."

"And do you know where all the rocks and ledges are?" they asked.

"No! But I know where they aren't," he replied.

Don't try to mess with Maine logic. It's a no-win situation.

All the talk of lobsters made us hungry for them...I know, we've eaten so many, we're turning brownish green and developing large claws in the front...so we went by the dock, picked out some shedders, waited for twenty minutes while they were steamed, and took them back to the boat for another fine lobster dinner.

Heidi and Jackson's flight left at 6:00 o'clock in the morning, long before the buses started to run. We arranged for a cab to pick them up at 5:00 on the town wharf. The airport was so close and so small, and the traffic so light, they didn't need the usual two hour lead time at the airport. We loaded their gear into the dinghy, in the dark, and headed in. At that hour, the harbor and dock were bustling as the lobster boats got ready for the day. We hadn't been on the dock for this early morning experience with the lobstermen before. They took on bait, fueled up, and piled extra traps on the stern. A diesel truck pulled up at the end of the pier with a hose run down to the float to fuel up each boat in turn. The bait was lowered down the wall in small barrels. The wharf was a beehive of activity. Amidst all this hustle and bustle, we said our goodbyes and shared hugs and kisses and looked wistfully after the cab as it took our daughter and grandson away.

With our guests safely on their way home, we returned to *Ceilidh* for a morning nap, a pre-breakfast nap. Being retired and on a boat, we shamelessly take a nap any time of day, even before breakfast...if we decide to. The rest of the day was spent washing, sending e-mail, and with a few final purchases as we prepared to leave Bar Harbor.

Chapter 20

Across to Nova Scotia

Each morning in Bar Harbor, we watched *The Cat*, the very fast jet-powered catamaran ferry depart for Nova Scotia. We succumbed to the temptation and decided to make a daytrip to Yarmouth on this exciting vessel. We were as interested in the ride and the boat as we were in visiting Yarmouth.

The alarm went off at 6:00 A.M. We dinghied in to the dock, pushed our way in to the crowded dinghy dock, walked to the village green, and caught the park bus to where *The Cat* docks, about three miles up the coast. We boarded the jet boat at 7:30 with six hundred thirty-three of our newest friends. The boat had seats for nine hundred passengers, located on a single deck, along with two snack bars, a cafe, a duty free shop and a brace of one-armed bandits. The vehicles, cars, trucks, and RVs rode on the deck below. Because of its speed of fifty-four knots, passengers must remain inside the cabin. This was a high tech boat with two movie screens and numerous monitors that show the navigation GPS chart and the boat's detailed progress for the entire trip from dock to dock. The airplane-like seats were quite comfortable. The food was moderately priced and of reasonable quality. By the time we boarded, each slot machine seemed to have already hooked a victim. The casino area had a weird music-like sound similar to what we had heard at the casinos in Atlantic City and on cruise ships. It seems they have developed a background sound that helps to stimulate gambling. The compulsiveness of the gamblers made it almost too nauseating for me to watch.

Clear of the boat traffic and out on the Gulf, *The Cat* accelerated to cruising speed, and we settled back for a fast, smooth ride. Its speed comes from four jet engines and a catamaran hull that skims across the top of the water. The speed was enhanced by a bulb-like extension on each hull which improved the entry to the water and increased the waterline length. Passengers were enclosed inside with little sense of movement or weather, much like the experience on an airplane. There was no sensation of the swells rising and falling beneath us. *The Cat* makes the one-hundred-fifty-mile trip from Bar Harbor to Yarmouth in two and three-quarter hours. To my surprise, I discovered Yarmouth is actually south of Bar Harbor on a course of 104 degrees. Depending on how you viewed it, you crossed either the northern tip of the Gulf of Maine, or the southern edge of the Bay of Fundy, both interesting and significant bodies of water.

The movie for the morning was *Finding Nemo*. Kids flocked to the aft section of the ship when it was announced and piled in on top of us. We made the mistake of selecting seats in the movie area without knowing they were front row seats for a kid's magnet showing. *Finding Nemo* was a fun movie with brilliant colors, a loud soundtrack and fast-paced, frenetic action. With the busy life below the sea, the chase scenes were multiplied ad nauseam. It helped pass the time and seemed a most appropriate setting as we jetted across the Gulf.

The passage itself had a significant air of unreality for boaters like us that usually move at six knots. The three-hundred-foot vessel was not bothered by bad weather. It was big enough and fast enough to push winds and waves aside and just go. We had to remind ourselves several times what was actually happening outside our enclosed cubicle as we flew across the open ocean at highway speeds. It was so different from our usual travel in a small sailboat moving at a fraction of the speed, that it was extremely hard to absorb and believe what was happening. The unreality was underlined when we arrived in Yarmouth on the southern tip of Nova Scotia in less time than it would take us to leave Bar Harbor, round the point of Mount Desert, and get to Southwest Harbor in our boat.

Yarmouth was a small town with an extensive fishing heritage. The wealth of the sea had always been its economic base. The town was struggling to tool up for its new role as the welcome port for two large tourist ferries, *The Cat* and the *Scotia Prince*. Aside from a nice new welcome/information center and several bus tours, its offerings were limited. The bus tours touted a dozen beautifully refurbished Victorian homes, built by sea captains during the town's heyday, and another tour developed by a group of residents who had parlayed their interest in gardening and presented their homes as flowering showplaces. A third mini tour took tourists to a few places like the lighthouse and the cliffs on the point. The ferry passengers who brought their cars and RVs usually left immediately for the trails of Nova Scotia, and for Lunenburg, Peggy's Cove, and Halifax. The full extent of the fishing fleet was not visible from the harbor, nor were the few private yachts. Next week the number of sailing yachts will increase dramatically when the first boats to finish the trans-Atlantic race from Falmouth England begin to arrive.

We found a seafood restaurant on the waterfront and enjoyed lobster and scallop crepes, accompanied by a glass of white wine. Yarmouth is the prime port for harvesting scallops from the Bay of Fundy. A scallop is the muscle connecting the two shells of a bivalve. Smaller bay scallops are found in sea grasses near shore, but large deep water scallops must be dredged from the sea floor by large ocean-going vessels.

We wandered through the town before joining a mini tour of the area. At the Forchu Lighthouse, our Acadian guide told of four teenagers who had driven out to the fifty-foot rock cliff by the lighthouse to watch the waves of hurricane Bob crash against the shore. A rogue wave, two hundred feet high, broke over the point, sweeping the four of them into the sea. Two were rescued, the other two drowned. The sea can be vicious. It's foolish to expose yourself to its fury at such violent times as an oncoming hurricane.

We bought a couple of shirts to remind us of our visit and enjoyed a glass of wine in the Thirsty Fisherman as the sun sank toward the horizon. We also tried a "ratty," a local dish made of roasted chicken and scraped potatoes, baked together in layers.

The pub's outside deck was closed. Someone had dropped a credit card down through a crack. They cleared the deck, pulled up some of the decking, retrieved the card, charged the dinner on it, returned it to the owner, and they all lived happily ever after. We had interesting conversations with several of the other passengers as we waited in line to re-board.

The trip back in the dark, again at high speed, seemed even more unreal than the one going over. I tried to imagine what it was like outside the immense cabin where the passengers were sleeping, watching movies and consuming all the fast food available. The huge craft, racing across the top of the waves, was in such stark contrast to a night at sea on *Ceilidh* that I really struggled to comprehend what was happening. I tried to envision myself in my 32' sailboat in the dark as this speeding craft bore down on me, wondering whether or not he was watching his radar and what might happen if he hit my small boat. I struggled to pull it together as a coherent scene and had great difficulty just trying. We arrived in time to catch the last bus back to town, back to the dock, and back to *Ceilidh*.

Chapter 21

Heading Slowly and Grudgingly South and West

We had visited with company, and they were gone. We had made a flying trip to Nova Scotia and back. Now it was time to begin our long trek in the general direction of Florida...very general and very long and very meandering. We didn't want to leave and begrudged that necessity.

The fog had returned, of course. Maybe it was the kind that might burn off by mid-day. The one thing I know about fog in Maine is that I know nothing about it. When we first awoke, the whole harbor was closed in. At breakfast it had receded just a little. After breakfast it had closed in again. Oh well! We needed a few groceries anyway.

We gathered our back packs and headed to the grocery store. We were trying to make do with what we could carry in our two packs. We actually succeeded and filled only the two back packs, if you don't count the two loaves of bread, the Doritos, or the nine-roll pack of toilet paper. We needed water too. We ran out again last night, but we were prepared with enough stored for the morning needs. The floating dock where we could water up had three fishermen on it who were catching nice-sized mackerel as fast as they could put their lines in the water. As we approached, they pulled in their lines slowly and a bit grudgingly. They understood the rules, boaters have priority access to the dock, but they didn't really like it. We filled our three tanks as quickly as possible and were off so they could return to fishing. The fog was still thick, but we could see almost a half a mile. That was not an abundance, but it was enough.

Since we were heading north and inland toward Sorrento Harbor, where the fog might have lifted, I hoped we would have enough visibility to see at least the opening between its outer islands when we arrived. The entry mark for Sorrento was on the

GPS, five miles away, across Frenchman's Bay. In the bay, in open water north of The Porcupines, we sailed in isolated splendor with a gray curtain drawn all the way around us. We sailed alone on our own private bay, at least that was the way it seemed. Islands on both sides, only two miles off, were invisible behind the misty curtain.

The GPS guided us straight to the red/white entry mark, and, by the time we got to it, we could easily see both the islands that formed the outer edge and the entirety of Sorrento Harbor as well. It was a cozy and well-protected harbor with a number of boats and very limited facilities. There was a dock with water and a phone, no shops, no groceries, nothing public, only some very spacious homes overlooking the water.

We carefully selected a spot to anchor in the midst of the moorings and dropped the hook. It's better to anchor with a chain rode in such conditions because you swing less and because chain requires a shorter rode, more in keeping with the scope of moored boats. Most of the craft in Sorrento were pleasure boats. There were lots of small sailboats. The lobster boats that supply the processing plant on the point were moored in full view, but on the other side of a bar that bisected the harbor. They even had a separate entry.

The first thing we noticed was the calmness of the water. We'd become so accustomed to the wakes of the boats moving about and the ocean swells coming over the breakwater at Bar Harbor that we'd forgotten life could actually be calm on an anchored boat. The second thing we noticed was the quiet. The clatter and clank of a busy working harbor and a tourist city had accustomed our ears to a noise that sounded oh so good when it quit. We spent a few minutes just enjoying the quiet and calm. It didn't hurt that these islands were among Maine's most picturesque at low tide with a height of rock exposed, backed by the ever-present stand of balsam fir, spruce and pine. We had lunch in the cockpit and brought out the pillows for a post lunch nap, the first one we've had in the cockpit for a long time.

The afternoon was spent in leisure pursuits. After supper, we went ashore and took a walk along the shore road. A couple that had just dinghied in from another boat, offered us a ride to Ellsworth to shop. They keep their boat here each summer and have a car. It was a gracious offer, but for the moment we were shopped up, so we declined. Three of the houses were old and large having been host to many a summer spent gazing out over Frenchman's Bay. A monument on the shore, a bronze plate fastened to a large granite rock, recognized those from the community who had served in the Great War. It was humbling to realize that some of the boys who had played under the apple tree that shaded the monument had lost their lives in Germany and France protecting our freedom. Each house had its well-tended patch of flowers that were blooming as if there was no tomorrow. Their tomorrows were limited since summer was nearing its end and the frosts of autumn weren't too far off.

The sun dipped behind a low-lying line of clouds that were scarcely visible in the haze of the late afternoon. That cloud line was probably the one the weatherman warned of, a strong, rapidly moving cold front with severe thunderstorms that was headed our way. We made mental plans of what was needed if we were stormed, but never had to put them in place. All we got that night was a light sprinkling of rain and the first really quiet night's sleep in a couple of weeks. We kept listening, expecting the wind to blow, but it never did.

Then next day we lazed a bit, had a breakfast of poached egg, grits, English muffin with guava jelly, cantaloupe, fresh blueberries and orange juice, a meal fit for a king and queen. The view from our private, floating restaurant wasn't shabby either. After this leisurely breakfast, we pulled the anchor and headed south, past Bar Harbor, between The Porcupine Islands and around Mount Desert to Southwest Harbor. NOAA, the National Oceanic and Atmospheric Administration, called for west winds, 10 to 20 knots. The wind sprang up as we were leaving Sorrento and quickly created two to three-foot swells on the bay. Despite our impressions of isolation from two days ago when visibility was limited, today we saw land all around. We were not as isolated as we thought. The mountains of Mount Desert rose from the water on one side in their sunlit splendor, while gray mountains far off in the distance covered our port stern. The cold front despite its benign passage had cleared the air and allowed the sun to shine in its Maine brilliance, making it a glorious day. As we surfed down the swells, the wind kept building,...10,...then 14,...then 18,...and finally 20 knots.

We passed Bar Harbor and headed down the coast of Mount Desert, the same one we had driven around in the past days, seeing the same landmarks, only now from the other side, from the water. The anabatic winds accelerated down the mountain side and the wind continued to increase, gusting to 25,...28,...30,...and 34 knots. The sea was covered with white caps making it much harder to spot the lobster buoys in the froth and foam. Steering was taxing as we struggled to spot the floats and miss them. With clear skies, navigating was easy. We could see both the marks and the land and everything else that was important for a safe passage.

Lots of boats were out on one of the prettiest days of the summer. But, increasingly, as the wind picked up, the only boats sailing were the ones headed east, down wind. Those headed west had doused their sails and turned on their engines. The ones that tried to carry sail in the gusty wind were over-powered and struggled to keep on course.

We turned west under the south end of Mount Desert and found ourselves plowing directly into the wind and the seas. The wind was so strong that it picked up the spray from the bow and flung it over the entire foredeck and straight into the cockpit. With the waves breaking on the nearby rocks, the coloring and grandeur of the mountains beside us, the spray flying over the boat, we felt like we were caught in a maelstrom of wind and sea.

We were glad to get to the protection of Southwest Harbor after only seventeen nautical miles. The Zinns had offered the use of their mooring at the head of the harbor, the end most protected from a west wind. The offer of a mooring was a welcome gift on this blustery day.

It was time to tackle a couple of boat jobs I'd been putting off. I drained the oil from the engine and suctioned it out of the transmission. I cleaned the transducer for the depth sounder to assure we get correct readings, and then I tackled the annual cleaning of the head hose. When urine and sea water combine, they form a calcification that builds up on the inside of the hose. In time, it blocks the hose completely. It's not a difficult task, but it's not my favorite either. I dismantled the head's pump and greased the piston. Two hours later, we had a new head, good for another year. Ah, the joys of messing about in boats! The alternative to working on the head, neglecting or ignoring it, is much, much worse. Don't even ask!

With the boat projects done, we settled down to a cup of tea, home-made shortbread, and baked salmon for supper. The wind gusted to thirty knots. *Ceilidh* bobbed and wove on its mooring, like a boxer dodging and taunting an opponent. It continued to blow until three in the morning, but we were tired enough to sleep soundly, knowing we were secure, tied on a strong mooring.

We talked about moving to Blue Hill Harbor, but we never overcame the "initial inertia" to get underway. Instead, we enjoyed the day reading and just relaxing. The sun shone brightly. The wind picked up again and blew hard, but in the early afternoon, it finally settled down to just a pleasant breeze. There was a lot of commotion with boats moving about, but we were tucked in a corner of the harbor and were not affected by all the activity. It was a true lay day, with most of it spent just lying around. I finished reading the mammoth biography of Winston Churchill by Jenkins. Churchill was a fascinating, complex man who stood tall at a crucial crossroads of history, earning a rightful place of honor.

The night was calm. The wind was still. *Ceilidh* and her crew sleep better in such conditions. The front had moved on, but it left behind the first cold of autumn. It was a two-blanket night with temperatures in the low fifties. High clouds covered the sky as we awoke. We had a few errands in town so we searched for the inner town dock on the north side of the harbor. As we dinghied toward the dock, we saw the rocks on either side, but missed the shallows ahead of us and the fact that they were blooming with seaweed close to the surface. The outboard prop wrapped itself tight and secure in the long strands of grass until it stalled. I was able to clear it with no more damage than a seriously chilled hand from reaching down into the cold, cold water. On the slow walk into town, we admired the small houses perched along the water's edge and the quaint Bed & Breakfast on the other side of the road. We tended to our errands and on the way back, stopped at Mrs. Spurling's front fence "market" and bought some homemade breads. The breads were just left on the wall with a sign showing the prices along with a small box for the money. We got underway to Swan's Island by mid-morning.

Chapter 22

Swan's Island

As we approached the green can at the exit to Southwest Harbor, a fishing boat pulled alongside and slowed.

"Hi *Ceilidh!* Glad to see you made it to Maine," the captain called.

We didn't recognize the boat and we couldn't see the captain very well. Okay, we thought, give us a clue. You obviously know us, but who are you and when did we see you last? The captain answered our unspoken questions before we could ask them.

"We rafted alongside you in Indian Cove last winter in Florida."

Then things began to click. He had come in to Indian Cove looking for water and supplies. There was no space at the dock so we'd invited him to tie alongside *Ceilidh* for a few hours while he shopped. We had also given him a cruising guide to the Bahamas. He had invited us to visit him in Maine this summer. We remembered he was from Maine, but had forgotten he was from Bar Harbor.

"Our mooring's available in Bar Harbor if you're headed up that way," he added.

How kind and generous. It was hard to keep the boats close together and hard to hear, so we shifted our conversation over to the radio. Mike was here in Southwest Harbor on a working boat for The College of the Atlantic. What a pleasant surprise, despite the fact that we're headed south, away from Bar Harbor and won't be able to accept his offer or enjoy his company.

The islands to the south appeared to be a single mass. It was impossible to separate them or to identify specific ones. We headed for a red mark on the GPS that was off the point of one island. We couldn't see the actual mark yet, it was still merged with the foliage. As we got nearer, the islands began to sort themselves out. All small Maine islands tend to look alike. It takes a compass, a chart, and a GPS position to assure you're passing the right one. Actually, if you're patient and wait, they take on definable shapes when you finally get up close, only then you can confirm that you're in the right place. Often times in life, we want to know what's ahead before it's ready to disclose itself. The truth is, we just have to wait until we get there. We're anxious to know things in advance, know what's expected, know what's the shape of things in the future. But life requires patience. It requires us to wait, to live with the unknown, to live today and not rush forward anticipating tomorrow. Tomorrow will come, but only when today is over. Islands will take on a recognizable shape when we get to them, but for the time being, enjoy the beauty of the mass of green and "smell the evergreens."

The skies continued overcast with darker clouds crowding the horizon to the northeast, possibly bearing rain? We left Two Sisters Island to port and headed toward the mark for the south entrance to Burnt Coat Harbor on the southeast corner of Swan's. The inner one of the two green cans puts you almost on the shore, but the current making the sharp curve has gouged it deep and we were able to pass in plenty of water. A lobster boat, coming out, thoughtfully passed us on the shore side, allowing us the deeper water next to the can since we have more draft. We picked out one of the green moorings belonging to the Lobster Co-op, and before we had secured the pennant and settled back on it, Everett called to us from the dock. He and Mary Katherine have a home here and had invited us to come visit. Everett was there waiting.

We met Mary Katherine and Everett on *New Love*, their Hatteras trawler in Venice, Florida, our first year of cruising. We've had some great conversations and lots of good times together. They extolled the beauty of Maine and invited us here. We've seen them almost every year since, in a variety of places. Most recently, we met them in Marsh Harbor in the Bahamas where they spotted us and hailed us on the radio. We had some nice visits there and they reiterated their invitation for a visit at Swan's Island in Maine.

We've kept in touch through e-mail and are now here to take them up on their offer. That's one of the joys of cruising, meeting people in different places and enjoying their company.

Everett and Mary Katherine took us on a grand tour of Swan's Island, a Maine vacation spot that has three-hundred-fifty year round residents and swells to over a thousand in the summer. We went to Round Stone Beach, quite appropriately covered with round stones. Next we took a walk on Sand Beach, a lovely white sand beach between two rock headlands. The access to Sand Beach is a walk through a sylvan glade coated with moss and bounded by evergreens of all sizes. The deer here are very friendly and unafraid of people. We saw one halfway up the steps of a house, asking for a handout, and there were six in another yard, two of whom had large beautiful racks.

As our tour continued, they introduced us to friends, an enterprising young couple who run a printing shop using an old style letter press with hand-set type. They craft greeting cards and have won numerous awards. We toured the local granite quarry which today doubled as a swimming hole with three little girls enjoying a dip in the fresh water. We stopped off at their nephew Timmy's lobster pound and bought lobsters and clams for supper. Timmy's eleven-year-old daughter was running the pound today and helped us select our lobsters from the floating box. Katie was not only very competent in running the pound, but she serves as "backman" on her dad's lobster boat, hauling and baiting the traps, the hardest work on the boat. When the Marblehead Yacht Club flotilla came into the harbor overnight, she took her skiff and collected and disposed of the garbage from each boat earning a dollar per bag. The lobster and clams Katie selected for us were tender and succulent. Full of good seafood and lots of happy memories, we found our way back to *Ceilidh* in the dark.

Everett picked us up for breakfast. Mary Katherine made the best pancakes I have ever eaten, loaded with wild blueberries. Instead of adding the berries to the batter, she sprinkled them on top just before she flipped them over to cook on the second side, you know when the bubbles showed all over the exposed side. We also had delicious raisin bread toast from a special bakery on the island.

Everett designed and helped build their house and boat house, located at the top of a rise, with a great view overlooking Burnt Coat Harbor. It was open and airy making full use of the view. Mary Katherine had a huge Luna shape on the porch filled with blooming flowers. In addition to lots of exceptional food, we had lots of great conversations while we ate and walked and enjoyed learning about everyday island life in Maine and Swan's Island in particular.

Point off Swan's Island

The year-round residents on the island have difficulties during the long dark cold winters. Mary Katherine and Everett have assisted many of them, helping them learn to cope with some of the problems peculiar to living on a small island in Maine. Everett has used his business skills to provide planning and backing to a local couple to help them get on their feet after an economic setback. Mary Katherine has helped several of the young wives learn to cope with the inactivity and isolation of a Maine winter. We returned to the boat with an admiration for our cruising friends for their role as good neighbors.

I could postpone it no longer. It was time to put on the wet suit and check to make sure everything under water on *Ceilidh*'s hull was in good shape. It has to be done every couple of months. In addition to the routine matters, I needed to check whether or not there was damage when the prop splintered the board three weeks back as we moved across Frenchman's Bay. The water temperature was in the high fifties, a temperature that can chill you down in a hurry. Happily, all that was required was a quick look that didn't take long to establish that the prop was okay and that everything was in good order. The only thing I needed to do was to change the sacrificial zincs that protect the prop and shaft from electrolysis. That took about twenty minutes, so I was soon back onboard, in the sunshine, in dry clothes, and warming up. We lazed in the cockpit and watched the harbor fill with sailboats, including a 70' schooner that "sailed to anchor." A push boat brought it the last few yards in to its spot. A push boat is a very small boat that is filled with a very large engine. The older sailing ships carried their push boat on board until it was needed to "push" the ship into place. Or it was sometimes used to power the schooner when the wind died. The passengers on-board the schooner for the week, seemed to be having a great time.

The Sabre next to us lists Memphis, Tennessee as its home port. They jokingly mentioned a long trip down the Mississippi River and all the way back up the East Coast to get here. They then admitted that they bought the boat in the northeast, are currently moored in Portland, and are impressed that we've come here all the way from Florida. "You're living our dream!" they exclaimed.

A dozen other cruising boats came in before dark, and then the *Victory Chimes*, a windjammer schooner arrived, sailed slowly into the harbor, around the point and anchored about 100 yards away. It was surprising to see all these transient boats in Burnt Coat. It was a beautiful, secure harbor, but there was virtually nothing to do ashore, not even a good place to get off the boat unless you have local contacts. A former restaurant was planning to reopen next year, but for now, there is little more to do than buy lobsters from the co-op, and tour the island on foot.

Mary Katherine had to leave to help her brother arrange and show his paintings at an art show at Christmas Cove. Everett wanted to pick our brains about the New England coast. Just this morning, he got a phone call asking him to deliver a recently purchased Catalina 27, from Portsmouth, New Hampshire to Amity, Long Island. It was his first delivery job. He completed his captain's license last year, qualifying him to make such deliveries of vessels. He hasn't traveled in this area and knew we had. We went over the charts with him, pointed out potential problem spots, good places to stop, and where to get fuel and supplies. After lunch, he showed us the cottage he and Mary Katherine bought and rehabbed for a summer rental. It stands on a rise with a view out both openings to the harbor, one of them watched over by a lighthouse. It had everything you'd want in a cottage in Maine. They did some clever modifications to the old structure that made it significantly more usable and comfortable. We'd really like to return and rent it some summer.

Since Mary Katherine was away, we invited Everett to supper on board. He knew Tom and Virginia Cabot, authors of a noted book about cruising in Maine on their beloved *Avelinda*. We read their book earlier in the summer. They lived on Swan's Island for a period of time. This is the second time our friends have referenced this sailing couple who did so much for the islands of Maine, to help preserve them in a natural state and make them available for all to enjoy.

Everett asked, "Do you remember the high winds Saturday night?"

"Of course!" we replied.

"Well, a 40' sailboat was launched that morning." Everett began. "They sailed into Mackerel Cove on the north side of Swan's. When they doused their sails, the motor wouldn't start. They quickly got an anchor down, a Bruce anchor with an all chain rode. About ten that night, near high tide, they started to drag in the very gusty winds, but before they could get a sail out or get underway, they were blown up on a ledge. There was a cabin nearby, so they waded ashore, knocked on the door, and by chance, they knew the people who lived there. Their friends invited them in and called for help. The rudder was badly damaged, so badly that they pulled it out and plugged the hole. I cut a wooden plug for them and someone else had some fiberglass and mat. Next morning the salvage boat put a line to the mast head to heel her on the side and then pulled her forward from the bow over both ledges and off, with only minor damage to the hull."

Stories like this remind you how close you are to disaster every day. We tried to learn from each situation in order to avoid a similar experience. It was important to realize that in a small boat, you live by the grace of the weather and the sea. You are never the sea's master. We had spent a most pleasant evening in the company of a good friend and were sorry to see him leave when we bade him good night.

The wind was calm, and we slept soundly until the lobstermen went to work about five in the morning. Our mooring was in line with the co-op dock where they load their bait, so one by one they passed close 'aboard on their way to sea. We repeated together, "We love to eat lobster. We love to eat lobster. We love the taste of lobster." Who wanted to sleep anyway!

Skiff and lobster traps

Chapter 23

Bucks Harbor

The skies were cloudy and overcast, but there was a small patch of blue spreading upward from the horizon. That was a good sign. We dropped the mooring and headed out through the maze of lobster trap floats. In the western entrance to Swan's was where we hooked a float four years ago. I wound up diving in the cold, cold water to untangle it from the prop. Today, we succeeded in dodging the floats, and I avoided a swim in the fifty-five degree water. However, I put so much focus on steering carefully between the maze of floats that I was distracted from navigating. As we passed Sheriff Ledge, I changed the chart book page and failed to see we had a little more distance to go up Toothacher Bay. I confused Sheriff Ledge with Hat Island Ledge without realizing it. Suddenly nothing made sense. The pattern of the marks didn't make sense. The distance to waypoints was off by several miles. My various navigational information didn't fit. Ahead on the right, I spotted a ledge, protruding above the water. According to the chart, there was no ledge there. According to the chart, you leave the first red mark to starboard, the next you leave to port, but that doesn't look right. We proceeded cautiously looking for other ledges, monitoring the depth sounder and using all our navigating tools to try to sort out where we were and what had happened. After a couple of miles of muddling along, the data popped into focus and began to make sense. The marks fit the chart. The bearings to known waypoints were right, and we identified Egg Rock, the one off the Casco Passage. At last we were "found." It was then that I realized I'd turned the page too early, and that was what caused the confusion. The good thing is that we made it through without "finding" any ledges with our keel. After several very unsettling minutes, happiness and sunshine returned to the captain and crew.

When we entered Eggemoggin Reach, the number of lobster floats diminished. A couple of dolphins swam alongside rolling up to breathe now and again. Dolphins in Maine don't seem to frequent the inner water between the islands as often as do their southern cousins. There are many, many more seals here this year than there were when we were here last. Either there are more around, or we've become better at spotting them. We looked longingly at the home of Wooden Boats as we passed. We'd love to stop, but it's not on our schedule today, maybe next time. We passed under the high bridge that crosses from the mainland to Deer Island. Bridges are a rarity for this part of Maine. There just aren't many. Access to the islands is by boat or by ferry.

Lobster floats

We headed for Bucks Harbor where we planned to meet Dick and Suzi. Bucks is their home port when they're in Maine. They maintain a mooring there. Bucks Harbor is a crescent shaped cove with a large island in the middle that provides good shelter from all directions. The Yacht Club welcomes visiting boaters, and there are some interesting places ashore. It is the kind of distinctive place that attracts cruisers. Dick said we could use his mooring until he arrived so we searched for it. When we found it, there were other friends tied there. They had engine problems and needed to be there several days. No problem! We'll just anchor in the eastern side of the cove.

We anchored and began to tape the toe rail and other bright work so we could sand and varnish. This time we'll do it like

Hinkley does. We can't possibly finish the whole project before the day cools but we can at least get started.

This is a popular harbor. Boats arrived in a steady stream all afternoon including nine windjammers with their passengers. A week's cruise on a classic schooner is a great experience, and they're obviously having fun. We overheard a passenger ask if it was okay to swim. The crew member said "Sure," without bothering to caution him about the frigid water temperature. The passenger dove in and surfaced with a shriek, shocked by the cold water. The whole anchorage chuckled when he climbed the ship's ladder, shivering.

A lapstreak launch powered by two oarsmen swung alongside the schooner and took the passengers ashore, in keeping with the old style of the schooners.

At dusk, as low tide approached, a large rock broke through the water close to our stern. We took in about ten feet of chain to shift *Ceilildh* forward a little. We were okay, but it was more due to luck than skill and planning. Another boat that anchored astern of us grounded and had to re-anchor. He didn't move far enough the first time and later had to move a second time.

When we awoke next morning it was raining so we stayed onboard. The forecast for tomorrow looked the same. Late in the morning it cleared a bit, so we went in to the local cafe for lunch. Actually, the cafe is part of the Bucks Harbor Market, an unusual small store that sells wonderful breads baked on site, live lobsters, produce, tennis balls. It rents videos and has a cafe out back. We had a nice lunch, made some phone calls, and bought some home baked breads. The sun peeked out late in the afternoon so we celebrated by going ashore again to get pizza for supper.

When we arrived at the café about seven o'clock, there was a long line and standing room only. Everyone had turned out not just for pizza, but to hear the local steel band which plays every Monday night. The steel band, I discovered, was the reason so many windjammers make port here on Mondays. Since there was no table, we ordered pizza to go and ate it outside, enjoying the island music. The band was quite good, with eleven steel drums, a keyboard and a rhythm player. The cafe owner perched on a stool in the abandoned brick fireplace just behind the band, playing the castanets.

Next morning as the windjammers raised their anchors and made sail, singing the traditional sea chanteys, we sanded in rhythm. Working in rhythm actually took some of the burden out of our sanding. Our varnishing project went well though it took three days. It's hard to get the sanding dust and debris off the surface when you're at anchor with no vacuum or a water supply to wash it away. But with plenty of time and close attention to detail, it turned out to be the best finish we've ever put on. Our teak certainly needed care. Meanwhile, we met new people, visited with Mike and Dawn on *Tanika* and returned several times to the local grocery for its bread, wild blueberries, and other good eats.

The cove is one of the prettiest we've been in. The songs of the birds echo against the rocks. The exposed rocks at low tide, are spectacular as well as menacing. The trees with their variegated greens are a changing kaleidoscope of patterns and the light piercing through them plays them like a stringed instrument, producing a symphony of ever-changing tints and hues. Mussels grow on the rocks just outside. Boats came and went. We met new people daily.

We reassembled the boat, refastening all the parts that had been removed for varnishing. It took longer than we had planned to locate the right screws and bolts for each parts we'd taken off. The sun hung around, making it another lunch in the cockpit day. We chatted with the skipper of a Herreshoff Bugeye, a fiberglass version of the Herreshoff twelve-and-a-half, as he literally sailed circles around us. He pointed out two bald eagles in a tall pine nearby that we had missed. We also spotted a Doughdish version of the same little Herreshoff on a mooring nearby. It was gaff-rigged, which I prefer. The gaff rig looks better balanced than a Marconi rig. This little green-hulled boat was in exceptional condition. I wish Herreshoff's classy little boat made sense in Florida, but it doesn't. The water is just too shallow.

Dick and Suzi returned. We had lots of catching up since we last saw them in Rockland, and they wanted to hear about our trip down east. They suggested that we sail together to Castine tomorrow, anchor off and visit Castine, one of the oldest cities on the east coast of the U.S. We agreed. We arranged to meet at the local eatery for pizza only to discover it was closed on Tuesday...and our mouths were all set for pizza. We've gotten very familiar with "Plan B" since we moved on the boat. Sailing requires lots of flexibility. There are other great things to eat besides pizza, especially since pizza is not available.

Chapter 24

Castine

There are not many lobstermen in Bucks Harbor but the ones there get underway and leave at dawn, tip-toeing out quietly. We barely heard them, and we felt no wakes at all. We're off for the fifteen miles to Castine after a swing by the yacht club dock to top off our water tanks. The yacht club is very generous with their water, asking only that you not use their limited supply to wash down your boat. Another day, another adventure. And on this fine sunny day, there was an unexpected adventure awaiting us.

A half-mile out of the harbor, *Ceilidh* suddenly lost forward thrust. The engine was running and in gear, but there was no push. I throttled back and eased into reverse. We were able to move backward, but we couldn't go forward. I opened the engine compartment and started checking. Dick and Suzi had moved on ahead so we hailed them on the radio with our news. I put on a wet suit and dove to check the prop. It was not fouled by any lines or debris, and more importantly, it was still there. A missing prop is a serious problem.

When Dick and Suzi came alongside Dick asked, "Is the shaft turning?"

Good question! It's always better to have multiple minds working to solve a problem. Bezy confirmed that the transmission flange was turning when the motor was in gear, but underwater, I noted the prop didn't move. Then when I turned the prop by hand, the transmission flange inside the boat didn't move. The shaft was loose and the prop was no longer connected to the transmission. On a second dive, I saw that the shaft had slipped out three inches. The problem was clear. The shaft had worked loose from the coupling that couples it to the transmission. I was relieved. Fixing a coupler is much easier than fixing a transmission. A coupler takes a day. A transmission could take a couple of weeks.

Dick offered to tow us back to his mooring where we could reinstall the coupler. Conditions could not have been better. The weather was calm. It was early in the day. The mooring was close by. In an hour I had the coupler installed and the shaft reconnected. We were elated at a quick and easy fix, made possible by having the necessary tools and parts on board.

After lunch, we again headed to Castine, but I noted that the shaft key was working out again. The coupler's key slot was too worn. It was time for Plan C. There was no mechanic in Bucks Harbor so we'll need to continue to Castine under sail, tacking to windward. We shut off the engine and put up the sails. Under sail, we struggled to clear the head of the cape with a dying breeze, and what little breeze that was left, was also backing and heading us. If that wasn't enough, the tide changed and began to run out, pushing us off our course.

Finally, despite the difficult, changing winds, we managed to just get around the cape and turned up toward Castine on a reach. The obstinate wind recognized we'd won, changed its mind, and began to help us by freshening a bit and providing an easy reach into the Harbor.

The day was marred by radio reports of a man missing from a boat in nearby Gilkey Harbor. Boats and divers were quickly marshaled for the search. The Coast Guard tall-ship *Eagle* was in the area and sent its small boat to aid. As the minutes ticked by without locating him, it was increasingly clear that hypothermia from the cold water would have taken its toll and that there was little hope of finding him alive. It was a harsh reminder of the dangers and the severe consequences of the smallest accident or mistake. Our coupler issue was of no consequence compared to this tragedy. It took a lot of the brightness out of an otherwise interesting day.

Dick and Suzi anchored near the float that held twenty small racing sailboats of the Maine Maritime Academy. Without power, negotiating both the wind and current under sail, we maneuvered to an appropriate spot nearby, and anchored. Dick and Suzi joined us for a glass of wine and a recap of the day before we dinghied in for dinner at Dennett's Wharf, finishing with blueberry ice cream of course.

Back aboard, I phoned my personal mechanic in California for ideas about how to proceed. Everyone should have a friend like Russ Fields who is knowledgeable and helpful in such circumstances. After listening to all that had happened, he concluded we needed a new coupler. The wind rose about midnight and kept us in constant motion the rest of the night.

It was time to plot and plan. After a bit of soul searching, I decided the best thing to do was to take the coupler off and show it to whomever I could find. If there's not a mechanic in Castine, we can sail to either Camden or Rockland, but we're in Castine, so let's try here first.

Eaton Boatyard was just down from the town dock in Castine. The first person I spoke with seemed very knowledgeable and showed me where my coupler's key-way was badly worn, and demonstrated why the coupler must be replaced. More than that, he was a Yanmar dealer and could order the part for delivery tomorrow. He was not satisfied when the person on the phone seemed hesitant identifying the exact part, so he requested she fax him the specifications to assure a perfect match. He couldn't have been nicer, or better informed.

It was only then that I realized he was not Kenny Eaton, owner of Eaton Boatyard, but an outside contractor from Bangor who works here in Eaton's a lot. When Kenny appeared, he said, "Shucks! We could get a coupler at Hamilton Marine, in Searsport. You can use my truck to drive over there if you want."

I decided to go with Kevin and the process we'd already started. It seemed more certain. But I was impressed by Kenny's generous offer.

Kenny is multi-talented and much in demand. As we were standing there, a man came up with a message from Kenny's cousin Anne.

"Anne flagged me down as I was passing her house and asked me to come tell you her hearing-aid won't work," the man reported.

"Okay," said Kenny, "I'll get out there and tend to it."

He's also very friendly and well liked. Dick reported, a few years back, there was a party on the dock with several boats gathered. They said, "Kenny, come join us!"

He responded, "I can't! My shirt's dirty."

"That's okay," they answered, "Come on anyway. You look fine."

Kenny thought a minute. Took off his shirt. Turned it inside out. Put it on again, backwards, and joined the festivities.

Kevin and Kenny work together easily. I'm in good hands. My part will arrive by UPS about mid-day tomorrow. I ordered all the bolts, set screws and shaft key as a set to be sure they would all fit together perfectly. "Right?"

In the meantime, I now had time to think about the dinghy floor. The inflatable floor had lost air during all the excitement yesterday. It was deflated and squishy this morning. A firm floor was necessary to help maintain the dinghy's shape and to provide a place to stand. The easiest solution was to pump it up, hoping the problem was the valve, and that the valve had come loose accidentally. I pumped it up and it held, at least it appeared to. I'll go with that until I know better. I much prefer simple solutions.

It was time to visit Castine, a city that has been under the French, Dutch, British and American flags since it was first settled in 1613. Its location was ideal. It had deep water access, a well-protected harbor, and direct land access to the forests that were so important in the first two centuries of European settlement in Maine.

When we got ashore, the first thing to do was eat. It was lunch time, and besides we were hungry. Castine Variety was formerly a very small drug store at the center of town, but changed to a slightly larger multi-service restaurant, small grocery, curio, and a little bit of everything shop. Today's lunch special was crab sandwiches, but they were all out by the time we arrived, just a few minutes after noon. We had to settle for lobster rolls. It was really tough when the second choice was lobster rolls. The rolls were piled high with lobster and with no, absolutely no filler. It was a feast. Of course, as was Dick's and my custom, we finished off with ice cream, choosing Gifford's, a Maine brand that is creamy and full bodied. We ate outside on a bench, in the sunshine.

As we ate, the cadets of the Maine Maritime Academy marched down the street shouting their cadence. Upper classmen ran on ahead to control traffic and to supervise. Their enthusiasm made up for whatever was lacking in style and crisp precision. They turned the corner and headed downhill to the waterfront for an afternoon of boat drills. The Academy has an excellent reputation and provides extremely well qualified men and women for the Merchant Marine.

The houses of Castine date from the 18th and 19th centuries. Most are well preserved. A printed guide for a walking tour provided information about each of them. The city had also protected their large old trees, oaks, maples and elms. These majestic plants created a quiet elegance and setting for the houses. Suzi picked up a leaf from a red oak, a rich, reddish purple one, and large enough to have provided a high degree of modesty for Adam and Eve. Unlike some older towns we've been in, there was a wide variety of style and structures due to the different national influences and varying time periods in which these houses were built. As a large natural harbor, Castine was settled early and then captured by each new power that came to the region. The town was built on a hill and laid out so each house would have a full view overlooking the harbor. The town looks like an amphitheater designed for the citizens to view from their houses the conflict and drama that was played out again and again in sea battles in the harbor.

Back on the water, the cadets of Maine Maritime Academy were learning to row lifeboats. Part of the drill was to maneuver close enough so they could throw water on each other with plastic scoops. The primary purpose was to learn to maneuver the boats in close quarters, but the secondary purpose of wetting down the opposing crew seems to have taken over. Other students took turns learning to drive a medium-sized launch. We were anchored in the middle of all this busy learning-mixed-with-frivolity and had no choice but to enjoy the fun.

Dick and Suzi invited us for hors d'oeuvres and wine on *Charles Ogalin*. This was the day when Mars was the closest to earth for sixty thousand years, but the clouds masked our view. We saw Mars when we were in Bar Harbor a few days before, but the boat's movement there made it look like only a strange squiggly through the binoculars.

The wind clocked to the south during the night and all the anchored and moored boats swung with it. The huge moored dock swung from a hundred feet in one direction to a hundred feet the opposite. It wound up right next to Dick and Suzi's boat. They awoke at one a.m. and found themselves close enough to step off onto the float from their side ladder. It was not a crisis, at least not yet, so they calmly pulled up their anchor. But there were a few related problems just to add a little challenge. The electric windlass quit working when there was still more than seventy feet of chain out. They had to complete the lift manually. And when the barge swung, it swung over their anchor. The anchor was now up under the float. They had to drag it out from underneath the barge and then pull it up. In doing so, they hooked a significant glob of heavy sticky mud. Struggling to remove the gooey mud in the darkness with only a brush and bucket finally convinced them they needed to install a wash-down pump to clean their anchor and chain without having to do it by hand. About two-thirty in the morning the anchor was finally out from under the float, back on board and cleaned. They found an empty mooring nearby and picked it up. After all the fun and excitement they'd had, it took them a little while to get back to sleep. Middle-of-the-night escapades are seldom fun, but they are usually memorable.

The UPS truck was scheduled to arrive at Castine between eleven o'clock in the morning and four in the afternoon. I wanted to get the coupler as soon as it arrived, so we went ashore just before noon, planning to enjoy another lobster roll while we waited. Alas! Today they were out of lobster, so we settled for more conventional fare.

Castine Variety serves all the locals who eat lunch downtown. The stools at the counter are always full, and finding space at the communal twelve-seat table is not easy. We found two chairs and struck up a conversation with a mother and daughter who have bought a house here for summer use. She was a novice sailor, so when she bought a small boat, the harbor master assigned her a mooring right in front of the yacht club "so they could keep an eye on her and keep her out of trouble."

Bezy visited with another couple who bought a 38' Alden, a classic boat that was a long time part of the community. It was such a favorite that everyone found it necessary to critique the sail trim each time they sailed. "Tighten up the luff." "The leech is twisted off at the top." "Tension the foot." She said it was very intimidating. That's what happens when an entire community has ownership of a boat, or at least feel they do.

Another table mate, a student from the Maine Maritime Academy, filled us in on the Academy. The freshmen who just marched past are today going to jump off the dock into the water. Tomorrow, they'll jump from the side of the training ship, *The State of Maine*. This exercise not only gives students experience, it helps motivate them to not repeat this experience and to stick with the ship until it's absolutely necessary to abandon it. The instructor is a former Navy Seal, so there's no question whether or not they'll jump. Our young friend is very proud of his school and of its outstanding record.

The coupler and bolts arrived at 2:45. Despite our efforts for an exact match, there were a couple of adjustments that had to be made for it to fit properly. There always are. We got the package off the truck, and then had to search for someone at Eaton's who would take our money. Eaton's was long on service and short on formal business issues. We finally found someone, paid for the part, and headed back to *Ceilidh* to install it. We'd like to make it to Belfast tonight, but time will be tight. It was five-thirty when the shaft, coupler and transmission were all properly connected.

Another front was expected to sweep through just about dusk, so we decided to remain here for the night and go to Belfast tomorrow. The Academy students came out to the float and launched their racing sloops for a series of races that lasted until sunset. Learning to sail is a required part of their curriculum, though most of them have been sailing all of their lives. The front wimped through with only a light sprinkle. Frontal passages are not consistent in Maine. You never know whether you're going to get a wimp or a howl.

In the morning, the clouds hung low and the sky was steel gray, the weather seemed to be sulking because of its missed opportunity the night before. *Charles Ogalin* went ahead to Belfast while Bezy and I stopped in Searsport to pick up a part we ordered from Hamilton Marine.

Chapter 25

Belfast, with a stopover at Searsport

We pulled in our chain...and then pulled in some more...and still more...before we finally got all one hundred twenty feet aboard. We're not accustomed to having that much out. As we left Castine, we checked our new coupler every few minutes. It was holding well. After a dozen checks, we finally relaxed and trusted it. Bezy and I each realized that the transmission was running smoother, even though we had not noticed it being rough. There must have been some minor vibration with the loose coupler that we'd just become used to over time.

There was a light fog lying down on the water. When it lifted, we could actually see Islesboro about three miles to port as we moved north, rounding the northern tip of the island. We've developed a strong affection for days on which we can see the land, other boats, and the marks. The water was glassy, even though the weather predictions called for 25 knots. Halfway to Belfast, however, cat's paws ruffled the surface. The wind began to build. Within fifteen minutes the wind had gone from nonexistent to 20 knots. Welcome to Maine where the constant is change, frequent, sudden change.

As we arrived off the town dock at Searsport, we looked for the Hamilton Marine moorings mentioned in the cruising guide, but they were nowhere to be found. Reluctantly we picked up mooring number fifty, an empty one up close to the dock. The whole area was somewhat exposed, and the swells were too bumpy to put the motor on the dinghy so I rowed ashore. Bezy stayed with the boat in case the owner of the mooring came back and needed us to move. The town dock was divided into "load and unload only," "local residents only," and a float that was taken up by a small sailboat and a lobsterman unloading lobster. A fourth option was another float to the side that had several dinghies pulled up to it with no sign saying who it was for. I chose that one. One of the dinghies was just leaving, so I eased into that space. There was no ramp from the float up to the dock, only a slippery ladder. I climbed up gingerly, holding on tight.

On the dock I asked directions to Hamilton Marine from a small group of men having a sandwich and conversing. "It's a mile or two to the left," one said. I thought it was a mile or so to the right but acquiesced to local knowledge. He noticed my wince when he said "a mile or two" and offered me a ride. I was glad to accept. After going left a bit, Scott, my new friend and benefactor, realized Hamilton must be the other way, a mistake much easier to correct by car than on foot. Hamilton Marine had the cabin lights I had ordered, and Scott waited the few minutes to take me back to the dock. It turns out that Hamilton does not maintain moorings anymore, which explains why we couldn't find one.

As we continued on to Belfast, the chart page changed just at the entrance to the harbor so it took a minute or two to piece things together and discover that we should leave the entry mark to starboard. Dick and Suzi reserved a mooring for us with the harbor master. They gave us directions to it..."astern of the red boat...near *Rejoice*, an Island Packet...the mooring with the orange pickup float." With such excellent information, we went straight to it. The windjammer schooner *Kathryn B* came in just behind us and anchored to provide "shore leave" for its passengers.

Belfast was a small town with interesting shops and a good selection of services for cruisers. Two assistant harbor masters were cruisers themselves so they understood our needs and made every effort to help. Diane was one of the assistants. We met her and Alex on *Ariel III* four years ago at the Seven Seas Cruising Association gam in Islesboro. They spent last winter on their boat in the harbor in Belfast. We don't plan to spend a winter aboard in a cold climate, but we are always interested to know more about boating, including how someone solved the various challenges of living aboard in extremely cold weather, with snow on the deck, keeping water from freezing, getting back and forth to shore, and keeping warm.

The crews of four boats got together for supper on *Ariel III*. It was a time of good food, good fellowship and lots of boat stories. Diane and Alex have two cats that are adventurous to the extreme. They jump ship when their boat swings close to other boat, then, rather than trouble the other boat's crew, they jump in the water and swim home. The crew hears the splash and quickly put on their "foulies" over "jammys" and row around in the dark trying to find the cats which by now have swum back home, climbed up their own personal cat ladder, (a large line with knots tied in it, something they can get their claws into), licked themselves dry, and snuggled down in their favorite combing box. The cats have other tricks as well to plague their owners and neighboring boaters.

Sue and Jonathan on *Rejoice* were from Freeport, Maine and were thinking about cruising. They hope to cast off their lines and start out when Sue retires in a year or so. Bezy and Sue spent a long time talking about living on a boat and what to expect

Jonathan and Alex suggested that a flexible coupling might help the problem with my coupler and shaft. A flexible coupling is a hard rubber insert between the shaft coupler and the transmission flange. It bolts to both and absorbs any shock from the propeller. It will also "sacrifice" itself by breaking apart to protect both the transmission and the prop if there is a severe jolt. Their comments started me wondering if part of my coupler problem stemmed from the board I split in two a couple of weeks back, or maybe the heavy wad of seaweed caught on the prop. If they weren't the cause, both events likely contributed, loosening the connection to the point that it finally failed.

When Alex and Diane were in the Bahamas, they noticed a snicker whenever *Ariel's* name was called on the VHF radio. After several days and a good bit of snickering, they finally cornered someone to ask about it. It seemed there was another boat named *Ariel* in the area. One day a call went out for the other *Ariel*. There was an emergency message for them. They were a long way away off in the islands, and it took a bit of doing with lots of relaying until they finally located the other *Ariel* at Conception Island. The emergency message then had to be relayed through the long chain of boats...repeated several times. The message which was heard by anyone who had their radio on was: "The surrogate mother is ready. You need to get your sperm to the clinic immediately." Finally hearing the story, they had a good snicker themselves.

The next day we were still enjoying the stories of our friends as we set about our tasks, washing, shopping and filling the propane tanks. The laundromat was just "up the hill." The grocery was just "up the hill." Propane was just "up the hill." So we climbed the hill. We had to do a "missionaries and cannibals" relay since we couldn't carry everything in the dinghy at once, four bags of dirty laundry, three small propane tanks, and two adults. And then, of course, we had to return with all of this plus three bags of groceries. The day was filled with comings and goings. Our folding two-wheel cart worked wonders but not miracles. We could load three boat bags of laundry on it. It held two propane tanks. We lashed them on with shock cords. After several trips back and forth, up and down, we had clean clothes, sheets and towels, our tanks were filled with propane, and we had fresh vegetables and other necessities for our larder. And I had even worked in a few minutes to use the land line at the harbor master's office to send e-mail.

Back on the boat, the Belfast River was running out. It held us sideways against the wind, and the swells began to bounce against our stern. I couldn't figure out a source of the swells. They weren't coming up Penobscot Bay. They weren't created by the wind, which was light, and besides, they were from a different direction than either wind or tide. I don't know where they came from. After a couple of hours they stopped. Dick and Suzi had noticed the same phenomena the previous afternoon, and they couldn't figure it out either.

Chapter 26

Islesboro and the Seven Seas Cruising Association Gam

Morning dawned crisp and clear. The north wind indicated a frontal passage had moved through during the night. We made our way across the bay to Islesboro and to Gilkey Harbor. Thirty-two boats were already anchored when we arrived. Kathy and Dick DeGrasse hosted a Seven Seas Cruising Association gam at their Maine cottage each summer. They reveled in the fact that there was space for the entire group to anchor in the water just in front of their house. We all went ashore for a pot luck lunch, meeting new friends and greeting old ones, a typical Seven Seas Cruising Association gam. This is the 13th annual gathering here. The program for the day was loosely organized with discussion groups on a variety of topics led by volunteers who have been to the places under discussion, or repaired and replaced the boat parts in question. With no dock and with large rocks across the waterfront, they rigged an anchor extending a hundred feet out into the bay, the other end was tied to a tree on shore. You tied your dinghy somewhere along the line, and a couple of boats ferried guests from the line, to the small landing area. The prize-winning dinghy name for the day was "Row vs. Wade."

We heard someone say "St. Petersburg" and introduced ourselves to Ted and Vicky on *Emerald Tide*, a Pearson 424 from St. Petersburg, Florida, where we're from. Ted had on a Metric Construction shirt so we played "Do You Know," and found we had many mutual acquaintances. We did a lot of work with Metric back when I was gainfully employed. We enjoyed a visit to their boat and they came aboard *Ceilidh* for a glass of wine. We toasted Pearson for the fine boats they built, and spent the evening talking about our boats and where we'd sailed.

At the gam, several friends urged us to apply for Commodore status of SSCA. We easily qualify with time aboard and miles traveled. Several people offered to sponsor us, and we decided to apply. We completed the forms and our sponsors signed them. Soon we could fly the red swallowtail burgee of a Seven Seas Cruising Association Commodore.

Chapter 27

Tenants Harbor and Earthly Heaven

For the first time the weather forecast focused on something other than rain and fog. A hurricane was rambling through the Caribbean. We could no longer focus on sailing here. We had to plan how to make our way down the coast and to Florida. We must figure out how to dodge the big storms and find places to put in when they threaten. Summer was over and Maine was beginning to pack up for the winter that would soon arrive. It was time to make our way south, to Boothbay, to Portland and the Isles of Shoals. We had had a most pleasurable summer with lots of old friends and with many new ones. Cruising in Maine is different. It is more challenging than other places, but more rewarding as well.

A slight haze filled the air and drew a misty veil over the mountains behind Camden as we exited Gilkey Harbor and turned south, headed for Tenants Harbor. There was no wind. It took longer than I expected to pass Camden. Finally, a light breeze freshened, on our nose, of course. Several Schooners were putting out from Rockland as we approached, their sails back lit by the hazy sun. One crossed just ahead of us. We were holding a constant bearing with it which meant we would collide if one of us didn't change course, so we bore off to go around their stern. The skipper was sitting behind the wheel telling sea stories. We were tempted to sail alongside for a few minutes and listen in.

As we approached Owl's Head, a small sailboat was caught in the current making very little headway. The breeze was light and his small outboard was "paddling" as fast as it could. There seemed to be more boats moving about today, getting in their last sail of the summer before they haul out for the winter. Boats of all sizes passed us. Was this the beginning of the migration south for the winter? Were these the boats we'll see along the Intracoastal Waterway and later this winter in the Marinas in Florida and the

Bahamas? The schooner *American Eagle* headed towards us, the sails out wing on wing. She looked elegant in her newly-sewn canvas. The lobstermen worked their traps on both sides. They have a lot more fishing to do. Their season is far from over. Were they glad to see the summer people go, or just going about their business in stoic Maine fashion?

We turned to starboard just before Southern Island, and entered Tenants Harbor. We found one of Cod End's bright yellow mooring buoys and picked up the pennant. We've come only thirty-three nautical miles and we're exhausted. Normally we would go much further in a day's run, but we're out of shape for such extended travel, spoiled by the short distances we've traveled the past couple of months. We considered a trip ashore for blueberry pie, but the gray skies outside and the warm snugness of our cabin tipped the balance. We opened the engine room door and allowed the heat from the engine to warm the cabin. We poured a glass of wine and pulled out a good book. The wind changed during the night, and the whole mooring field swung the opposite direction, rearranging everything without incident, in rather close quarters. Tight mooring fields always amaze me. I am amazed at the way boats adjust to the "close order drill" that a mooring field requires without any help from their captains.

We called Beth to confirm that we'll make it to Otis Point today. She was our benefactor in July who rescued us from the rain and took us home with her so we could wash clothes. We've kept in touch by e-mail, and she insisted we stop by on our way south. Today's trip is a short one, around the point, past Port Clyde, up the St. George River to Otis Point, and to Earthly Heaven. But first, we had to pay for our mooring and take on some water and fuel.

The first three miles south of Tenants Harbor was in open water. Surprisingly, there was a noticeable swell from the northeast that followed us until we rounded Mosquito Island and turned west toward Hubble Island and Port Clyde. The lobster traps were much thicker in this area than they were on the way up. With warmer water inshore, the lobsters were moving out into deeper, cooler water. There didn't seem to be any toggles attached to the floats here which made it easier to navigate. We have made it this far without snagging a float. It would be sad to catch one now, and in addition the water has gotten colder so to have to swim to free the prop would be even more unpleasant.

St. George River was wider than I expected. We migrated naturally to the starboard side going upstream. It wasn't really a conscious decision, more force of habit. I'm just accustomed to driving on the right hand side of the road and keeping to the right. I looked over to port and there were lots of floats on that side, but very few where we were. We had made a good decision to hold to starboard, rather, we lucked out and stayed on that side out of habit.

Otis Point was about four miles farther. Now the trick was to recognize Beth's house from the water. We eliminated several houses because of a variety of features that didn't fit, and then spotted what looked like a good possibility. The skylights in the roof confirmed we were right. Mica, the large black poodle barked to announce our arrival, and Beth came out to the dock braving the chill wind to direct us to her mooring. The pennant had some kelp and a colony of mussels growing on it, a sure sign that it needed more use.

Just to the north was a strange-looking barge with floats extending almost to the shore. Beth explained, "It's an aqua-culture project for growing oysters. They have reduced the growing time for oysters from four to two years." That's a huge improvement in bringing a crop to market.

Beth welcomed us warmly and immediately insisted that we plan to stay several days in order to recover from the onslaught of bad weather and to let her pamper us. She was very persuasive. It was very tempting. She had baked a berry pie with blue, black and raspberries in it, just for us. She marked the crust with "B and C" in our honor.

"I picked the blackberries and the raspberries myself!" Beth said. "They grow right here on the property."

I hadn't picked blackberries in a very long time, and I wanted some to top my cereal in the morning. "Is it all right for me to pick some?" I asked.

"Why not?" Beth answered as she pointed to the bushes behind the garage. So I picked a big handful of blackberries. It was thirty-six years since I had last pulled blackberries off a prickly vine with their long thin stems stretched out to hook my shirt with thorns. Back then, I was sweating profusely and scratching chigger bites on a farm in Tennessee. In the future, I think I'll pick my blackberries in Maine.

Hurricane Fabian was powering up the Atlantic and might affect us over the weekend. We checked the charts for possible places we could anchor if its remnants move onshore and race northward over the land. The most likely effects of Fabian would be high surf and large swells that could reach out hundreds of miles in advance of the storm. Here in the river, we would be fine if Fabian heads this way. I need to check the weather channel for more information before we finalize our plans.

When we first arrived, it was a gray dismal day, the same kind of weather we had had when we were here before. But in the afternoon, the sun burned away the clouds and shone brilliantly through the spruce and birch. I used the sunlight and took a number of pictures, including a couple of *Ceilidh* hanging on the mooring, framed by the tall spruce trees on the shore. We drove to Port Clyde for ice cream to go with our berry pie, and pork loin to have with the rice for dinner. We were well fed, relaxed and happy. We decided to accept Beth's invitation to stay another day.

Beth had to take her car for a seventy-five thousand mile check-up to a mechanic whose shop was seventy miles away. "Just make yourselves at home," she said as she closed the door behind her.

We started the day lazily with hot showers, make that very long, luxurious, hot showers. I had forgotten how nice a really hot shower was. It had been awhile.

Last evening when we had talked about popovers like the ones we had at Jordan Pond, Beth's face lit up. "I love popovers," she said. "We'll have to make some."

She had produced four different recipes and a special pan for cooking them. I offered to give it a try. I donned my baker's hat, selected the recipe that billed itself as "fail-safe" and soon was up to my elbows in flour. The ingredients were straightforward as was the process. The only thing out of the ordinary was that you heated the pan in the oven before you poured the batter in. My first ever popovers emerged from the oven properly risen and golden brown. We spread them with butter and raspberry jam for a virtual feast.

We picked up lobsters and mussels for dinner. We remembered Beth's recipe for lobster, steam them in sea water with seaweed for flavor. The mussels were likewise steamed, but in white wine with shallots and garlic. She added a pat of butter and a dab of cream to the "liquor" she'd cooked them in and used that for a juice dip. They were wonderful. Salad, bread and another round of pie a la mode completed our feast.

The weather channel indicated that the hurricane had slowed and begun a turn to the north. The storm's barometric pressure was up a half-inch. It had also lost twenty knots of wind speed, from 140 miles an hour, down to 120. It was expected to pass close to Bermuda before swinging harmlessly out into the North Atlantic. Its impact on us would be indirect, high surf and large swells out on the Atlantic Ocean but no storm winds. The swells should arrive Saturday and Sunday, hundreds of miles in advance of the storm itself. It would likely affect our passage, maybe even hamper our attempt to make it to Portland. But before we worried about getting to Portland, we first needed to get to Boothbay. We planned to leave in the morning.

At first light, about 5 o'clock, I looked out toward the river. Our room had a side wall of glass with a floor to ceiling view of the river, overlooking Andrew and Betsy Wyeth's home and the mountains of Camden. I saw none of that. This morning I saw only a curtain of gray fog, thick, dense fog. Rain fell steadily and the wind was up. I rolled over, pulled the covers over my head, and went back to sleep. This was not the right time, nor were these the right conditions in which to venture forth.

Beth greeted us with hot coffee and biscuits and urged us to stay another day. It didn't take any urging. I dinghied out to *Ceilidh* in the rain to power up and charge her batteries. And today was the day for Mika's trip to the doggy beauty parlor, again, about 60 miles away. Everything here was "at a distance." When you live out on a peninsular, you have to go a-ways to get to anywhere.

We lazed around the house, kept up with hurricane Fabian on the TV, and checked out the new tropical storm developing in the Gulf of Mexico named Henri. We'll have to deal with that one about a week from now. The fire in the fireplace was warm and inviting. It was the right day to sit around doing nothing, just watch the fire burn and figure out a possible strategy to deal with the two storms that were in our path.

After supper, our conversation ranged far and wide, cruising in the Baltic Sea, raising a family in Switzerland, adventures in fog, and living in Maine.

"And how would you sum up your summer in Maine?" Beth asked. "We've had an unusual amount of fog and rain. Did it cause you lots of trouble?"

"Not really," I replied. "The fog was frustrating at times, but it was a good experience to learn to handle a boat in the fog. We have so much better instruments on a small boat than they used to have. Maine fishermen have gotten around in fog for decades. With radar and GPS and an auto helm and a depth sounder we ought to be able to handle it. We learned to let the auto helm steer. It's almost impossible to keep a straight course in the fog when you have no reference point to steer by. The auto helm doesn't have that problem. The rain was a nuisance at times, but we have good rain gear so we just went ahead."

"Have you had a good time?" Beth inquired.

"Yes, indeed," Bezy said enthusiastically. "It's been even better than we imagined, and we expected it to be pretty good. Maine is spectacular, weaving between the islands, smelling the trees, watching the waves break on the rocks, and...eating lobster, and mussels, and blueberries, and ice cream, was scrumptious. We had a great summer in every respect."

"Lobsters have been the major issue of our summer, the good and the bad. Trying to miss the lobster traps bedeviled us. We enjoyed meeting the hardy men and women who fish for them, and it was fascinating to learn about the process of trapping them. But the best part was to pick the meat from the shells and eat them."

"....dipped in butter." I added.

After all the conversation about eating, we went to bed with visions of lobster claws dancing in our heads.

To my dismay, when we awoke, we were again ensconced in early morning fog. As we showered and dressed, it started to slowly recede down the river. Beth cautioned that although it might be clearing on the river, at sea it was likely still hanging around and might do so for the entire day. We didn't want to overstay our welcome, and it was important to get south before the cold set in, but we don't want to get caught out in serious fog either. We factored in as many possibilities as we could and decided that we should go.

Chapter 28

On to Portland and...

We left bravely at eight o'clock, after many thanks, lots of hugs and a wistful look back at Earthly Heaven. It was up for sale, so we would likely never be back. But Beth has a condo in Florida, and we promised to take her for a sail this winter where it is warmer. People and friendships are much more important than places, even very special places.

The fog was still thick but we could see at least as far as the opposite bank of the river. All we had to do was dodge the lobster floats and the connected toggles. The toggles were tracking with the outgoing tide so they were lined up with our course, heading down river. That made it easier. The lobstermen were out circling slowly as they pulled their traps. It seemed like it was going to be a good day, until we passed the islands and looked ahead at the "fog wall" stretched across the entrance to the ocean. Once again it was back to radar and the GPS. We could see the sun on top of the clouds, trying to break through. It gave us hope. It also illuminated the fog in the distance. But at the surface and where we were, the fog was still just dense, dense, dense. The next buoy appeared on the GPS. We steered towards it, while keeping a close watch of the rocks alongside us. The lobster boats seemed to make smaller blips today than previously. Mostly, they seemed to be stationary near a buoy as if holding in a known position until the fog lifted. At least they're expecting it to lift, I thought. We've noted this same phenomena several times. Lobstermen tend to get to a safe position away from traffic and just sit until the fog lifts and they can go on about their work.

As we approached Pemaquid Point, two east bound sailboats conversed on the radio. They were very close by. I tried to raise them on channel 16, the hailing channel, unsuccessfully. I called a "Securite" on the radio and announced my position and course. Then they suddenly appeared only a boat length to our port, in the tight confines of the ledge off the point. They ghosted past and quickly disappeared astern.

I entered a waypoint for Fisherman Island, and we determined a bearing to steer for. The green can off Thrumcap showed on the GPS. Bezy spotted a kayaker scurrying across the channel, headed for Fisherman Island. He was hard to see through the fog and had no radar reflector. He was very vulnerable in these conditions. We hoped for his safety.

We identified the three red marks that form a triangle, kept them all to starboard, and headed past Squirrel Island into Boothbay Harbor. Just as we drew alongside Squirrel Point, we suddenly emerged from thick fog into bright sunshine. Fog is a strange phenomenon.

In Boothbay Harbor, several boats were heading out to sea. We wondered if they knew what conditions were like outside? As for us, we were glad to be headed in, headed toward a mooring that would hold us in place and free us from responsibility of moving when we couldn't see...at least for the night. We had considered going all the way to Portland today, about fifty miles total, but when the fog closed in yet again, Boothbay was the unanimous choice of both captain and crew. Even Swiss Chocolate, our teddy bear mascot concurred, and Swiss is a daredevil.

There were a number of empty moorings in the harbor. Labor Day weekend was really the end of the season here. Tugboat Inn had already shifted to a "seasonal rate." We walked around a bit in the shops, bought a couple of sweatshirts and some ice cream and settled down for the evening. There were lots of chimes and bells in Boothbay. A church or perhaps the town clock, it was hard to tell, but one of the large clocks chimed ships-bells at four o'clock. It was the first time I'd ever heard the distinctive ships' bells chiming the half hours of the watch on a public clock. It was a nice touch! A seal swam close to the dinghy showing no concern for us. We've seen them almost every day all summer, in a wide variety of locations, in the open ocean, in harbors and in the channels. Hurricane Henri moved ashore on the West Coast of

Florida. Fabian battered Bermuda with 120-mile-an-hour winds. The surf on the ocean was rising. NOAA forecasted 5' to 8' swells for the next day. There was a lot going on, but for the moment, for tonight, we were snug and cozy on a mooring in a very protected historic harbor.

The next day, we really wanted to leave for Portland, but was that a good decision? There were protected areas on both ends of the passage which would be no problem, but there was also a stretch of twenty miles of open water in the middle, exposed to winds and swells off the Atlantic. The buoy reports at seven in the morning indicated swells of 4' to 5' for that critical middle section. The sun was shining brightly, with no fog. That was the best news. We decided to give it a try. The Cuckold's rocks where we turn west toward Portland, had waves breaking over them, with white spray flying high into the sky. A small boat was fishing nearby, despite the small craft warning for the day. *Ceilidh* is not considered a small craft. She was designed for open water and coastal cruising, so that warning was not a concern for us.

We rounded the mark and headed west, exposed to the open ocean swells and winds. For a while we were protected from the southeast by outlying islands, but when we moved beyond their protection, the swells rolled under us at the forecasted 4' to 5' or higher. They were, however, long ocean swells with gradual, sloping sides that lifted the boat up gently as they slid under. Visibility was good except for a hazy mist which lay low on the water, the mist that the sun struggled to clear away. This last hint of fog finally receded as we approached.

Surf was breaking on Sister's Island ledge. We could see it more than four miles off. It showed as a line of white froth just off our course on the port side. A minke whale rolled on our starboard bow. I called for Bezy to come up from below and see. She stuck her head out the companionway in time to see its second roll, and then it was gone. They are such large, gentle creatures. You feel no threat, only awe, and a sense of privilege to share their world with them.

A red nun buoy marked each end of the ledge. These marks showed where it started and stopped allowing us to pass safely with confidence. As the water shoaled, the swells increased as the ledge squeezed them. Mounds of water surge upward reaching eight feet in height, but they are still the long, rounded ocean swells, easy to handle, not breaking waves.

All was going well until we approached Cape Small and Fuller Rocks just off the southeast end of the ocean passage. We must pass through a narrow cut between the cape and the rocks, and the chart shows only eleven feet over the ledge where we cross. Subtract the trough of a four-foot swell and that leaves only seven feet on top of the rock ledge. Seven feet was a minimal clearance for *Ceilidh*'s keel, especially in such turbulent conditions with large swells rising and falling. In addition, we couldn't see the opening. All we could see from a distance was a continuous line of breaking froth with the foam and the turbulent water flowing all the way in to the shore. There was probably a space, a little calm water somewhere along the line, but it was certainly not visible from a mile off. Unable to be sure of the narrow opening, and with concerns about the depth with the rise and fall of the swells, we decided it was best to go outside, around Halibut Ledges and Fuller Rocks, in deeper water, rather than attempt to pick our way through the swirling, turbulent waters, hoping to find a hard-to-identify channel. The longer but deeper path's the choice for me, not the straighter one with a possible, most unpleasant kind of encounter with a granite ledge. We've managed to avoid the ledges all summer, that would not be a good way to end our visit.

We picked up the Webster Rock's Lighthouse, and set a course for Brown Cow buoy, past Drunkard Ledge. The seas were breaking over Drunkard Ledge, as mounds of water pushed up, flashing green as they crested, and then shattered into a white foam cap as they toppled over themselves and dissolved into flat swirls on the other side. It was a show of awesome power surging so close by. If we were swept into it, it would smash our boat to small pieces in a matter of minutes. We marveled at the power of the ocean and its grandeur as we sailed steadily and safely past, a couple of hundred yards off. We soon reached the protection of the islands, and sailed on past Cliff Island.

Approaching Peaks, we passed nearby Hussey Sound which was the headquarters of the U. S. Navy's North Atlantic Fleet during World War II. Peaks Island was heavily fortified and the pass to the northeast was closed off with submarine nets. Today, there are no warships, no shore batteries, and no steel cabled nets. The boats of today were all built for pleasure or work, and the people out on the water were enjoying the bright sunshine of one of the last boating weekends of the fall, not worrying about enemy warships.

The Centerboard Yacht Club in South Portland welcomed us back and had a mooring available. We had come only thirty-five nautical miles today, but it was a challenging trip and tiring. After a brief nap, we took the launch over to Portland and walked down to Hamilton Marine to buy a flexible coupling for the connection between our shaft and transmission. Like any dutiful boater in a marine store, I never bought just the thing I came for, I also found a collection of other things to buy, a new plug for the dinghy, two safety lights for the life jackets, a new flashlight, two crotch strips for our life preservers and a round of zincs to protect the shaft, strut and rudder bearings. I returned from Hamilton's with my backpack full of stuff.

Since visiting Peaks Island at the beginning of the summer, we had discovered that Bezy's cousin lives there. He is a cousin she has never met, one she didn't even know she had until very recently. Her parents were in their fifties when they adopted her and she was almost a full generation younger than all her cousins and is still finding ones she hasn't met. We've been in touch by phone and arranged to meet him today.

"We're the fifth house down from the cupola on the bluff atop Peaks. You can tie your dinghy to the first dock," Bill said.

The directions were somewhat confusing from a distance, but once we saw the place, it all made sense. Patty, her cousin's wife was waving to us before we got our anchor down. We anchored in the exact same spot we anchored in in July when we were here for the Peaks Fest. Their grandsons were in the parade. One was in the pie-eating contest that we watched. They made block-print T-shirts. They ate blueberry pancakes as we did. We were together, maybe even rubbing elbows, but didn't know each other at the time.

Bill and Patty met us at the dock and welcomed us to their home atop the high bluff overlooking Portland Harbor. They've remodeled an old inn with an expansive view of the harbor. Each room had large windows with a great view. The dining room/entry area had a lofted ceiling. The whole house was open, airy, bright, and inviting. From the porch you needed only to shift your eyes to take in the whole panorama of Portland Harbor, boats entering and leaving, ferries plying their routes to the islands, and tankers from all over the world docking to discharge their oil and other cargo. Bill's father can sit for hours watching all the activity.

Bill and Patty invited John Flint, a neighbor and former harbormaster to share a glass of wine and to regale us with stories of the port. He's a typical Mainer with his terse, matter-of-fact answers. I asked him, "Why do the lobstermen use toggles on their trap lines?"

"To catch the yachtie's props," he replied. He then added, "The toggles are visible at low tide in case the primary float is lost."

Bill and Patty moved here eighteen months ago. They plan to live here nine or ten months of the year, and then winter in Florida. Bill's parents love it here and have their own special rooms. Like many islanders, they keep a car in the parking lot over town and take the passenger ferry across once a week for groceries and a variety of errands. Bezy and Bill swapped family information and got acquainted. They started to fill in the gaps left empty by the years they had missed.

Bill told of an uncle who was devastated when his wife died suddenly. He couldn't face living alone so within days of his wife's death, he took out his high school annual, identified all his female classmates who were single and wrote to three of them proposing marriage. Two agreed. He accepted the response of the one with the earliest postmark and sent the other a very valuable Stamp

Collection, worth fifty thousand dollars, as a consolation prize. He and his new bride lived together happily the rest of their lives.

Bill and Patty were most gracious hosts, warm and loving family. We made plans to get together again soon, perhaps in Annapolis, or maybe in Sanibel. We went back to *Ceilidh*, rejoicing with our newfound family.

The next morning we moved back to the Centerboard Yacht Club, returned to a mooring, and began to prepare for the trip south. Dick and Suzi were moored nearby and joined us for wine and cheese. We wanted to hear about their trip here from Belfast and how they handled the difficulties they had had with the fog. We all agreed emphatically that navigating in fog was exhausting. We made a motion and approved it unanimously to banish all fog for the rest of the trip south.

As we talked about our summer in Maine, it seemed the right time for a toast.

"Raise your glasses and join me," I proposed, "To Maine and her incomparable variety, her exquisite rugged beauty, and to the magnificent summer she has provided us."

"Shouldn't we toast the challenges too?" Dick asked. "We've had a number of those."

"Yes, let's toast them also. We got through all of them pretty well. They seemed more a test of patience and a learning opportunity rather than a fearsome danger," I responded. "Taken with all the good things, they pale in comparison. So here's to the challenges. We learned from them and survived them all."

Bezy added, "And let's toast our friends, both old and new, all those who welcomed us and shared so generously their homes and their hearts. Oh, and to the unknown friends who have shared their moorings. Everywhere we went, everyone was so kind and generous and caring. We were welcomed so graciously."

Suzi said, "I'd like to toast all the great food, the fresh-baked breads, the wild Maine blueberries, the mussels and clams, and above all the delicious tender lobster."

"And the ice cream," Dick added. "Don't forget the blueberry ice cream...all of it."

"And," Dick said, "I'd like to toast the Friendship Sloops, those stout boats, and the hardy people who sail them. It's a privilege to be associated with folks like that."

"And the people with whom we sailed, Bill and Kathy, and John and Carole...And all the great sailors of the Ocean Cruising Club, and of the Seven Seas Cruising Association. Here's to them. It's always a pleasure to get to know other cruisers and spend time with them," I added.

"I'd like to toast the balsam trees that smell so good, the trees who've donated their needles for my pillow to remember Maine by," said Bezy. "I still remember the first day we realized we were right next to that island by smelling the trees when we couldn't see a thing in the fog."

"I think we need a special toast to the lobsters," I said. "Day in and day out we shared the water with them, with those who trapped them, and dodged the trap floats, and of course ate them. It's as if we spent the entire summer with lobsters, one way or another, living and sailing with them. Here's to the lobsters!"

"Oh! And the Old Man, we mustn't forget the Old Man," Suzi exclaimed.

Sailors for centuries have honored the Old Man of the Sea, seeking his favor and asking for a calm passage. The sea is a demanding task master that stretches you to your limits. It is also a seductive mistress that woos you by its soothing rhythms. It can be both gentle and ferocious, but neither a seductive mistress nor a task master can be controlled. A wise sailor knows that and never ventures out without showing his respect for the Old Man.

"The Old Man likes a tot, he does, a tot of rum!" said Suzi.

We got out the rum and ceremoniously poured a tot into the water. "For the Old Man!" we said together as we raised our glasses one last time.

The constant movement of ferries, fishing boats, sailboats, power boats and even the *Scotia Prince* kept us rocking with their wakes until after dark, and then the harbor finally settled down for the night and we slept.

It's time. The weatherman has put together a forecast of five consecutive days of bright sunny weather. He claims, "A high will build in to the area from the northwest with clear skies and no rain." Fabian the hurricane has accelerated into the distant North Atlantic and dissipated. Henri has blown itself out over the land. It's time to head south, down the coast, past Portsmouth and the Isles of Shoals, past Boston, Scituate, and through the Cape Cod Canal. It's time to leave Maine with its rough-hewn, hardy, gracious people, its untamed rugged coast, its delicious lobster, mussels, and blueberries, and the fascinating pithy comments made in unique Mainese. It's time to take our venturing to other areas. We cannot leave, however, without promising ourselves to return. The magnetism of its tough reality bewitches us as well as the friendliness of its people. We'll always be "from away," but from time to time we can at least be back "here."

About the Author

Clifford A. McKay's lifelong apprenticeship in sailing began when he was eleven years old, and he was the first boy to sail the now world famous Optimist Pram in Clearwater, Florida. He sailed a wide variety of boats in the ensuing years. After serving thirty-seven years as a Presbyterian Minister, he retired and purchased a thirty-two foot sloop named *Ceilidh*, sold his house, furniture and car, and set sail for new adventures afloat. For the next eleven years, he and his wife, Bezy, sailed their Pearson 323 from the Bahamas to Maine, meeting fascinating people, reliving Colonial History, and reveling in the challenges of small boat cruising. He wrote and shared his adventures by e-mail with a wide range of friends and family. He is blessed to be the father of three children and married to a wife who shares his love of sailing. They live in Fort Myers, Florida.

Both Clifford and Bezy are commodores in the Seven Seas Cruising Association. He is also a member of the Ocean Cruising Club.

His articles on sailing have been published in *Southwinds Magazine* (Jan, 2010 - May 2012), and his supplement on the Origin of the Optimist Pram is included in *History of the Optimist Dinghy 1947 - 2007* by Robert Wilkes.

Clifford has a BA from Emory University, a MDiv from Union Theological Seminary, Richmond, VA, and a MA and PhD from Vanderbilt University. He published a theological work for his PhD.

He sailed in early Southern Ocean Racing Circuit competition, Midget Ocean Racing competition, the Junior Snipe Nationals and crewed on a racing yacht, returning it from Maui to Seattle.